BOTTOM-LINE PROFITS

BOTTOM-LINE PROFITS

How Ordinary Entrepreneurs Create Significant Wealth In a Decade or Less

ISBN (paperback): 978-1-964046-26-6
ISBN (hardback): 978-1-964046-30-3

Expert Press
www.ExpertPress.net

The information provided in this book is for informational purposes only and is not intended to be a source of advice or credit analysis with respect to the material presented. The information and/or documents contained in this book do not constitute legal or financial advice and should never be used without first consulting with an insurance and/or a financial professional to determine what may be best for your individual needs.

The publisher and the author do not make any guarantee or other promise as to any results that may be obtained from using the content of this book. You should never make any investment decision without first consulting with your own financial advisor and conducting your own research and due diligence. To the maximum extent permitted by law, the publisher and the author disclaim any and all liability in the event any information, commentary, analysis, opinions, advice, and/or recommendations contained in this book prove to be inaccurate, incomplete, or unreliable or result in any investment or other losses.

Although the author and publisher have made every effort to ensure that the information in this book was correct at press time, the author and publisher do not assume and hereby disclaim any liability to any party for any loss, damage, or disruption caused by errors or omissions, whether such errors or omissions result from negligence, accident, or any other cause.

Content contained or made available through this book is not intended to and does not constitute legal advice or investment advice, and no attorney-client relationship is formed. The publisher and the author are providing this book and its contents on an "as is" basis. Your use of the information in this book is at your own risk.

Editing by Elaina Robbins
Copyediting by Wendy Lukasiewicz
Proofreading by Geena Barret
Cover design and book design by Paperback Expert

BOTTOM-LINE PROFITS

How Ordinary Entrepreneurs Create Significant Wealth in a Decade or Less

Brian Basinger, CPA

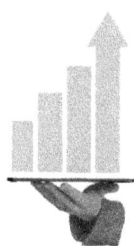

Contents

Introduction

I often think of entrepreneurship as a journey through the wilderness. Sure, it's easier to stay at home, but where's the fun in that? There are rivers to be crossed, mountains to climb, and boulders to overcome—a landscape filled with obstacles.

As you're traversing this treacherous path of entrepreneurship, a good financial plan acts like a map. It lets you plan for the obstacles ahead so that when you get to them, they're non-issues. You knew they were coming, and you're prepared to face them. Your financial plan creates this relatively smooth path toward success.

Conversely, lacking an understanding of finances and taxes does the opposite; you're left blind to the roadblocks. The same obstacle that might be a non-issue for someone who understands money—not just money broadly, but entrepreneurial finances—could be the thing that derails someone without that foresight.

As an entrepreneur, you probably already have faith in entrepreneurship. I certainly do. Entrepreneurship benefits individuals, the country, and the economy as a whole. It has transformed my life and the lives of the many business owners I work with. I hope it's already transforming yours, but I wrote this book for those who could be doing a little better.

This book isn't for Elon Musk and his ilk. It's better suited for entrepreneurs who have a real business but have stalled out and feel like they aren't getting what they expected from their business.

Maybe your business isn't profitable enough. Maybe you're getting killed with taxes. Maybe your business makes you feel trapped, or you're heading toward retirement and don't have a way out. You may be making $250,000 to $750,000 per year, but you feel stuck, plateaued, and overwhelmed. You're looking for guidance because you know things could and should be better, but you don't know what you don't know, and you need guidance to know what to fix and how to fix it.

If that sounds like you, *Bottom-Line Profits* will provide you with a practical tool kit and clear instructions on how to use your finances to help you succeed. I'll cover everything from large-scale goal planning to the minutiae of tax strategy and accounting. You'll have a fully detailed map that will guide you to your entrepreneurial destination: bottom-line profits.

1

The Profitable Mindset

If you're a podcast person, check out thought leader Russell Brunson's podcast, *The Marketing Secrets Show*. In one episode, "The Drifter vs the Driven," Brunson discusses two kinds of people. "There are two camps of people, and I had different names for them," he explains. "In *Atlas Shrugged*, Ayn Rand defines the Chupacabra as the prime movers and the looters. Napoleon Hill, he talks about it [too] . . . It is essential for us to be able to figure out where we are at and how to shift . . . *There are people who are driven and people who are drifters.*"[1]

What's the difference between the driven and the drifters? I think it comes down to having a clear long-term

1   Russell Brunson, host, "The Drifter vs the Driven and Live Q&A with Russell," *The Marketing Secrets Show* (Podcast), June 20, 2022, Accessed August 29, 2023, https://marketingsecrets.libsyn.com/the-drifter-vs-the-driven-and-live-qa-with-russell.

vision and specific goals to serve as milestones along the path toward that vision. Drifters lack a clear vision, and as a result, their goals (if they have goals) often feel arbitrary and lack the "why" behind them to drive the sacrifices and actions necessary to turn goals into reality. Driven people, on the other hand, have a clear vision, thus allowing them to create specific and meaningful goals.

We can't pursue things that aren't defined for us or are abstract and intangible. If we're engaging in such an approach, it means we're drifting, passively observing whatever happens to cross our path.

We're all guilty of this to some degree.

"I wish I could travel more."

"Wow, I wish I could afford that car."

"Wouldn't it be nice to have a lake house?"

"I wonder when I'll finally have a comfortable nest egg for retirement."

How often have those kinds of thoughts drifted across your mind? We all have a long list of mental wishes, but we tend to push them away. Beaten down by the realities of life, we start to think that we're not going to achieve those lofty dreams. We surrender our grand aspirations, assuming they're beyond reach.

No more. This book is about bottom-line profits. And to get there, we have to clarify what you want to achieve and why. It's okay to have big financial dreams for yourself and your business. Your financial dreams can happen. They don't have to remain vague desires; they can become concrete objectives. To manifest those dreams of success, we have to quantify them so that we'll know what to do to achieve them. That's what this chapter will cover.

In the following pages, I'll guide you through the steps that will pinpoint those dreams of profitability for your business and for yourself. When you identify what your dreams mean to you and how much capital you need to live the life you want, you can then generate a number and a plan to make those dreams a reality. I want you to get specific about what you want, understand why you want it, and learn how to formulate a plan to leverage your business to achieve it.

What Is Success?
Bear with me while I get a little philosophical. In this section, we'll delve into three main components of success: financial freedom, control over your destiny, and time (the ultimate luxury). We'll also take a look at a writing exercise that will help you figure out your priorities when it comes to success.

Financial Freedom
Motivational speaker Brian Tracy summed up the concept of financial freedom when he said, "In psychology, money is what is called a 'deficiency need.' . . . Put another way, when you have enough money, you don't think about it very much. But when you have too little, you think about it all the time." [2]

---

2   Brian Tracy, *The 100 Absolutely Unbreakable Laws of Business Success,* (United States: Berrett-Koehler Publishers, 2002).

When you don't have money, its absence becomes palpable. Money is all you can think about. For many people, dwelling on financial worries is a prolonged agony, stretching across years and even decades. They constantly think about money because they don't have it. It's difficult to imagine what it would be like to not worry about money, let alone grasp how freeing that would be. If you've spent a lifetime gasping for air, breathing easy is almost unthinkable. But that's what financial freedom is—breathing easy.

Financial freedom is the ability to live your desired lifestyle. It means living the way you want without producing income through your work or pinching pennies. The number that constitutes financial freedom is different for everybody, but I want to assure you that it's an achievable goal for normal, ordinary people. Financial freedom isn't just for Harvard alumni or the rich and famous. There's no reason why you can't replicate the same accomplishments as many of my clients—regular folk whose businesses took off thanks to having the right financial map and a lot of elbow grease.

Control over Your Destiny

When I sold my first company, cryptocurrencies were just taking off. With no real understanding of these digital assets, I invested $50,000 in a crypto fund. A total FOMO (fear of missing out) moment. I felt like I had to participate. Of course, crypto started crashing right at that time, and the fund collapsed. I couldn't even choose to ride out the downward trend and wait for the market to turn around. I was along for the ride, in no way in control of my destiny. The fund sent me the remains of my investment—around $12,000—and I learned a valuable lesson about investing in areas where I have zero control.

I want to contrast that story with my first boss, Roger. Roger owned a slew of businesses in fields that he understood and had decades of experience in. He knew his businesses inside and out. He could look at the financial reports and know exactly what was going on, and then he could tell his team what levers to pull to resolve any issues.

Roger came in once a week for staff meetings. All his expertise and knowledge told him everything he needed to know about what was going on in this business, so he was able to drive it without giving it much of his time. He had financial freedom, and he was in control of his own destiny.

Control over destiny isn't the same thing as financial freedom. Financial freedom means that you're confident in the money that you have because you know how to create it, you know how to protect it, and you're not blindly relying on a boss, a stockbroker, or a stroke of luck. Do you feel you're running your business in a way that allows you to control your destiny? Or are you subject to the whims of fate?

Obviously, we're all somewhat subject to outside factors like the economy. But think about it like this: If you're not in control of your financial destiny, you're a passenger on a potentially sinking ship. You have to sit there and watch the ship take on water, hoping the crew knows what they're doing. Either way, you're along for the ride. But if you have control over your financial world because you run it and understand it, you're no longer a passenger—you're an experienced, respected captain who keeps their cool in times of crisis. You don't control the ocean, but you can steer in bad weather and sail into the sunset.

Time

You've likely noticed that a major component of financial freedom and control over destiny is time. You're successful when you can use time the way you want, not have other people dictate it. This doesn't mean you're not engaging in activities but that you can choose to impose constraints on your own time.

Many a CEO chooses to stay involved in their business with fewer hours, for instance, once they reach a certain threshold of success. Hate paperwork? Despise spending hours answering emails? Financial freedom means you don't have to suffer through those tasks anymore. Other profitable entrepreneurs sell their companies and start up a second career as an artist or homesteader. They worked hard doing something gainful, and now they get to pursue their passions, lucrative or not. Still, others may choose to retire and pursue hobbies or spend time with family.

A life of leisure doesn't suit everyone—especially those with an entrepreneurial drive. I know this from experience. After I sold my first company, my idea of freedom was huge chunks of leisure time. I was doing a lot of family stuff, spending time with my kids, and engaging in hobbies. But it didn't fulfill me. Don't get me wrong—I truly value my kids, my family time, and my personal interests. They just weren't enough. I wanted to work! To create things. To explore novel goals and challenge myself in uncharted territories. So I did, and now I feel fulfilled, even though not every moment of the day is fun.

Defining Your Successful Lifestyle

Now that we've considered financial freedom, control of your own destiny, and time as components of a successful mindset, it's time to get personal. Grab a pen and paper, or pull up a document on your word processor, and put your thoughts in writing. Or, if you prefer, record a voice memo. I do this exercise with all my new clients, and it works surprisingly well.

Close your eyes and picture your successful self. Visualize your surroundings, and hear, smell, and feel everything. Then answer these questions:

- Where are you?
- What objects, structures, or natural features surround you?
- Who are you with? It could be people you know or types of people.
- What kinds of activities fill your time?

Your answers should create a vivid mental image, something we can start with to discover how much you need to live that dream. Your successful number is going to be very different if you picture yourself in faraway Dubai versus a lake house half an hour away from your current home. So take some time, examine your feelings, and then get ready to pull out your calculator.

How Much Money Do I Need to Live My Dreams?

Now that you know what being profitable looks like, it's time to make a plan. I use a simple three-step process with my clients: (1) figure out how much you need, (2) figure out how much you currently have, and (3) create a plan to make up the difference, if there is one.

How Much I Need

I have developed a specific process to help my clients figure out how much money will make their dreams a reality. When coming up with the annual dollar amount, you have to consider all kinds of expenses, including housing, health care, food, debt, payments, transportation, vacations, and discretionary money. This may seem difficult to calculate, but it's easier than you think.

If you're like most of my clients, you have an idea of what your mortgage payment and car payment are. You have a general inkling of how much you spend per year on things like groceries and travel. An estimate is okay for the calculation; it doesn't have to be perfect.

This is a lot to think about, so you may find it helpful to consult your accountant to usher you through the process and help you calculate your number.

Future Financial Net Worth

After you've figured out that dollar amount, multiply it by twenty. I'm not joking. This is your future financial net worth—the net worth you need to support that successful lifestyle.

Why do you need that much? Multiplying by twenty assumes a 5 percent rate of return on your assets. Five percent is a safe rate of return that doesn't force you to put your assets at significant risk. That rate of return securely funds that successful lifestyle. So if you need $100,000 a year to support that lifestyle, you would need a net worth of $2 million to earn $100,000 per year using that safe 5 percent rate of return.

How Much I Have: Current Financial Net Worth

Calculating how much you currently have is a multistep process. You have to consider your personal assets and liabilities, which will involve adding up a lot of numbers. Then, a little math will show you exactly where you stand.

Financial Assets

Your current financial net worth isn't how much you're making right now; instead, it's your current net worth. This is an important distinction. Current net worth can be divided into two categories of assets: personal assets and financial assets.

Personal assets provide personal benefit but not financial benefit. A personal asset doesn't put more money in your pocket in the short term. For instance, let's say you have a vacation home. You don't rent it out; it's a sanctuary for you and yours, but it's not earning any money. It may be gaining in value, but on a monthly or yearly basis, it's not making you income.

Financial assets, on the other hand, actively put more money back in your pocket. That's another important distinction because when we calculate current financial net worth, we only include financial assets. That's right. You wouldn't count personal home or vehicles or anything like that. You only count assets that are producing income. Income is the key here.

The most common financial asset for an entrepreneur is their business. How much is your business currently producing in annual cash flow? Anything else that is producing income on a regular basis—rental properties, stocks that produce dividends, among others—is also considered a financial asset.

Liabilities and Calculation

Once you've figured out all your assets, it's time to look at liabilities, including personal liabilities. This includes any type of debt: a mortgage, business loan, credit card debt, student debt, you name it. This might seem unfair. If your personal house isn't a financial asset, why is the mortgage included as a liability? Because you have to pay that mortgage every month even as the house isn't actively producing income.

Next, you subtract your liabilities from your financial assets. That's your financial net worth as of today. Subtract that from your future net worth as calculated in the last section, and you've got your magic number.

How Long Do I Need to Amass Wealth?

To meet your definition of successful, getting the money overnight would be nice. Unfortunately, that's not how life works. So how long does it take to amass the necessary amount of money for people to live out their dream lifestyle? And what can you do to truncate that time?

Most financial advisors will tell you that it takes thirty to forty years of receiving a paycheck and making investments to create a good amount of money for retirement. Following that plan, you may not be able to live out your dreams in retirement, but maybe you'll have enough for the expected remainder of your life and can survive until you die.

Do you like the sound of that? Me neither. The problem with this approach is twofold. First, thirty to forty years is quite a while. Second, you don't have control over what happens during that time span. You're at the mercy of the market and your financial manager; you're nothing more than a passive participant.

In this scenario, you need up to *forty years* to amass wealth because you're not getting a good rate of return. But if you can increase the rate of return, you can achieve wealth in a much shorter period. I always try to help my clients reach their magic number in *less than a decade*.

To determine the rate of return, calculate the gap between your current net worth and the net worth that you need. At my firm, we usually have a calculator handy to do this.

For the sake of simple numbers, let's say your current net worth is zero, and you want to get to the magic number of $2 million in ten years. You'll need to invest $35,000 per year with a rate of return between 30 to 40 percent. Only one vehicle will get you that kind of a rate of return, and it's your business.

If you have a business that runs like a well-oiled machine, you have the ability to use your expertise, leverage other people's time and money, and control the outcome. Nothing else hits all three of those points. This unique combination allows you to achieve the necessary rate of return and to transition from where you are—even if you're starting from zero—to your desired destination in ten years rather than forty.

Bottom-Line Profits: Not Just for the Elite

As we wrap up this chapter, I want to tell you a little story. My client Aaron runs a successful commercial cleaning business. Aaron was one of my first clients, so I had a front-row seat to watch his inspiring story.

"I was trapped in a job I had no love for," he told me when we first met. "I knew I had no future there. I was also dealing with a divorce and was at a pretty low point in my life. One day, as I got ready to go to work, I realized I couldn't continue down this path. I didn't want to keep investing my time and energy into a company that I didn't care about and that didn't care about me. I was already getting one divorce, so why not get another." He laughed. "Whatever happens, this was a time to reset. Even if it meant living on a diet of ramen noodles, I was willing to embrace it."

"So why cleaning?" I asked.

He shrugged. "I didn't have any extraordinary skills, and I didn't have a head start or good connections. So I did something I knew how to do: clean up messes."

Aaron opened his cleaning company and began by tidying up apartments for college students in preparation for their meticulous white-glove checkouts. He brought in less than $20,000 that first year, leaving him financially stretched. He was, indeed, subsisting on ramen noodles.

The path he followed wasn't rapid, yet things got better as time went on. The next year, Aaron managed to generate $48,427 from his business. At that point, he realized apartment cleaning had a low ceiling. He pivoted to cleaning office buildings. The company's revenue climbed to $87,262 by the following year. Aaron continued to build his business in steady, seemingly unremarkable steps.

By his eighth year in business, Aaron had built this venture into a million-dollar enterprise. He successfully sold it for seven figures and transitioned into real estate and diversifying his endeavors. He now actively engages in multiple businesses and real estate undertakings, manages a spectrum of projects, and loves every minute of it. He definitely reached his profitable number and then some.

I don't know how you got into entrepreneurship, and I don't know how your business is doing right now. But for Aaron, success wasn't a story of groundbreaking innovation or revolutionary concepts—it was a simple cleaning and janitorial business. That's not the most creative idea in the world. Aaron wasn't doing something that had never been done before, and if you're like most of my clients, neither are you. What Aaron did do was keep a flexible business model that turned toward opportunity and provided quality service. And, of course, he hired a financial advisor who helped him implement much of the advice you'll read in the subsequent chapters of this book.

Maybe you wish your bottom line was a little different right now. Maybe you're wondering what to do about your impossible workload or dwindling sales. Aaron's story shows that entrepreneurship is a tangible path for financial success for almost anyone, and more often than not, financial freedom can be achieved in less than ten years. Aaron did it in eight.

If you performed the exercises in this chapter, you now know what success means to you, and you know how much you'll need to get there. Now all that remains is for you to strengthen your empire. Let's optimize your business so you can reach that financial goal in a decade, rather than decades. In the next chapter, we're going to look at efficiency—a fundamental aspect of keeping a business healthy.

2

Efficiency

A few years into running my accounting firm, I was the classic busy entrepreneur getting pulled in a hundred different directions. Like a lot of entrepreneurs, I was using my time inefficiently and failing to prioritize. I always felt like I was in an emergency situation, and I barely glanced at my own finances, except to make sure I had enough cash to cover payroll and expenses.

On October 15, 2017, I was finally getting around to preparing my own tax return. I'd once again inefficiently used my limited time putting out fires. I'd filed for an extension, and I couldn't put it off anymore. That was when I realized that while I'd helped countless clients with tax strategy, I hadn't done tax strategy for myself. I watched in horror as my tax bill kept going up and up to the tune of $10,632. This was the same week as payroll. Paying both payroll and that tax bill nearly wiped out my entire account.

That weekend, my wife had arranged for the family to go on a hike. It was a beautiful time of year, and my children were small and in a good mood, but I couldn't enjoy any of it. I walked along like a zombie, thinking, *I'm a chartered professional accountant. I'm supposed to know about money and taxes. Yet here I am with almost no money in my account, having gotten hit with a $10,000 surprise tax bill. How did I get here?*

The pain of that experience prompted me to make a lot of changes in my firm. I set aside time every week to look at my finances. I made sure I was being intentional about everything that was happening and that I wasn't letting stuff sneak up on me. The goal of this chapter is to help you avoid my situation entirely. Efficiency is the way to do it.

This chapter will teach you to pick out the most meaningful key financial indicators by which to manage your businesses on a day-to-day, month-to-month, and quarter-to-quarter basis. It's all about efficiently using numbers to help you make decisions in your business and stay on track to reach your goals. I know it's not realistic for entrepreneurs to dig into every transaction, especially once things get going. But the idea is to pick out the critical few numbers that need to be looked at to help drive better decisions.

I'll talk about tax strategies more in chapter 5, but here you'll find the entrepreneur's practical guide to, in a limited amount of time, efficiently locating the financial numbers that are most important to controlling your business on an ongoing basis.

Three Key Efficiency Concepts

An entrepreneur's success often hinges on the ability to clearly perceive reality and act decisively. But amid the hustle and bustle, it's easy to lose sight of the bigger picture or overlook critical details (like your own tax strategy!). We've all been there. That's where the magic of efficiency comes into play.

Numbers are more than digits on a balance sheet or financial statement. They are your business's silent storytellers, revealing hidden truths and providing insights that can be transformative. Even if you're not a math whiz, numbers are your secret weapon for efficiency. They can help you make informed decisions and steer your venture toward success.

In this section, we'll explore the three key efficiency concepts you'll need to abide by as you look under the hood of your business. We'll dive into the profound impact of numerical truths, measurement, consistency, and a data-driven mindset in enhancing your entrepreneurial journey.

Numbers Reveal Reality

Are you familiar with the optical illusion called "My Wife and My Mother-in-Law"? Originally created by an anonymous German illustrator in 1888, and later made popular by cartoonist William Ely in 1915, the image is all about perspective.[3] Looked at one way, you see an old woman in profile with a bulbous nose. Looked at another way, you see a young woman with her face turned away. The inability or ability to see both shows how subjectively you perceive reality.

What does this have to do with entrepreneurship? As an entrepreneur, you have a lot going on. Naturally, to avoid drowning, you probably tend to focus on some things more than others. You don't always see the full picture or see it from all angles. I know I do this.

That's where numbers help you. Numbers help you see reality and reflect it back to you in an undeniable way. They provide a different angle than what you subjectively perceive as you go through the daily motions of running a business.

Examples of this abound. I could probably point to any business owner, but I'll focus on myself. When I started to get into my numbers and really focused on them, I realized that while my sales were increasing, my profits weren't increasing as much as I thought. When I got a new client, I thought we were bringing in money and taking care of that client. I focused on the high of getting more business and trying to do a good job. I failed to look at the other angle.

When new clients signed up, I would make compromises with payment schedules and spread them out to make it easier on the client. This became a problem. So much of the work was front-loaded, so I was incurring higher costs on

3   "My Wife and My Mother-in-Law. They Are Both in This Picture - Find Them," Prints & Photographs Online Catalog, Library of Congress, n.d., https://www.loc.gov/pictures/item/2010652001/.

my side, both in terms of my time and my team's time. I was incurring those hard costs up front in the form of payroll. Bringing on new clients, though good in the long run, was creating cash flow problems in the short term. I wouldn't have known this if I hadn't started consistently looking at the numbers. The numbers revealed that hidden image.

What Gets Measured Gets Improved

The idea that numbers reveal reality leads into "what gets measured gets improved." This is a time-tested, true statement. Stick a number in front of you and focus on it, and you'll take actions to improve it. If you don't know what the number is or fail to pay attention to it, you won't improve it. The measuring itself doesn't improve anything, of course, but shining a light on the details causes you to pay attention and take action. That's what improves the numbers.

Let's use sports as an example here. Sarah is a runner with an upcoming race. She meticulously logs her daily running times, heart rate, nutrition, and sleep patterns as she trains. Sarah soon notices that her heart rate during training sessions consistently spikes too quickly, so she adjusts her training plan to incorporate more varied workouts. Her cardiovascular fitness improves, and when race day comes, she beats her previous record by quite a bit. If she hadn't bothered to track her heart rate, Sarah never would have beat her time.

Consistency Is Key

When it comes to efficiency, consistency is key. Most businesses conduct a quarterly or monthly review of their finances, which is better than nothing, but with that much time between reviews, it's hard to be consistent. Work piles up, and it takes more time to conduct reviews that are spaced further apart. Problems may have gone undetected for too long. Entrepreneurs should be reviewing their numbers *weekly*. At the bare minimum, monthly. Create a weekly recurring calendar reservation and get it done.

A weekly review of numbers doesn't sound fun, but it doesn't take much time. I've managed finances for multiple companies that have gone over seven figures in annual sales, and I manage my finances myself. Yes, I'm an accountant, so I have some advantages there. I dedicate one hour a week, and my most successful clients, whether accountants or not, are doing the same thing.

Now, there are plenty of things I don't handle personally. I'm not doing my own payroll or keeping up on daily detailed tasks. But because I spend an hour a week on finances, paperwork doesn't accumulate and become some giant project I have to take on. That small window of weekly time allows me to deal with issues as they come up instead of waiting.

Even if you employ a bookkeeper, you need to do the review because it's your own money that's involved. For a bookkeeper, a number is merely a number, a task on a to-do list. They may perform dutifully, but I guarantee they don't care as much as you do. It's not their money.

One time I was talking to my client Jeff, who had a successful business. We were reviewing numbers when he shook his head and went off on a bit of a tangent.

"You know, I used to come home and have a glass of wine at the end of the day," he said. "It was my way of relaxing and forgetting about the day."

"Used to?" I asked.

"Yeah, things changed when my business took off." Jeff smiled. "It wasn't because I had a drinking problem or anything like that. I didn't quit drinking altogether. That wasn't the point. I was using that glass of wine as an escape from whatever negative thing had happened during the day, from the problems I had."

"Huh," I said. "That does make sense. I think a lot of people do that."

"Well, when I realized this pattern, I made a decision. I told myself that whatever problems I have, I need to stop trying to escape them. I need to attack them, push harder on them, not back up and give them space to grow. That was the catalyst that made my business take off."

That conversation stuck with me because sometimes that weekly review can feel terribly negative. It's like staring into a mirror for too long—you see your failures and your inadequacies all too clearly. It's not pleasant, and it's definitely natural to want to escape that. But the more you face your problems head-on, the more you can go about solving them and get results that make you feel better.

That's the real concept here with consistency: doing it every week. It's probably not going to feel good, especially at the beginning. You'll uncover some unsightly truths. I'm right there with you. The key to consistency, whether you've allotted an hour or ninety minutes, is to make that review a rock-solid appointment. However far you get in that time is enough; don't go over your limit. If you do that every week, you'll see realities that you wouldn't otherwise see, and then you can do something to effect change.

Four Crucial Measurements for an Efficient Business

We've got our key efficiency concepts: numbers reveal reality, what gets measured gets improved, and consistency is key. Now it's time to decide what you'll be consistently measuring so you can reveal realities. The short answer? There are four areas I recommend you monitor to improve business efficiency: cash flow, sales, expenses, and customer satisfaction. We'll take a look at each of these in turn.

Cash Flow

Have you heard the cliché "cash is king"? It's 100 percent true. Without cash flow, your business won't work. That's why cash flow is number one on our list of efficiency metrics. I recommend you have a detailed picture of what the next four to six weeks will look like, with a vague projection of your cash flow about a year in advance.

The worst time to seek money is when you're desperate for it. When you're in a pinch, you're vulnerable. You're at risk of either accepting unfavorable terms and high interest rates from banks or making frantic calls to clients, pleading for immediate payments. Seeking funds when you're in dire need, at the moment you need them, is far from ideal.

That's why, when it comes to securing cash, foresight is your ally. Ideally, you want to spot the need for additional funds well in advance. While a week's notice isn't great, it's certainly better than suddenly realizing you'll be out of cash tomorrow. So if you conduct that weekly assessment that includes your cash flow, you'll gain the ability to identify longer-term trends and address issues well before they escalate into emergencies.

The core concept here circles back to the introduction of this book: using a "map" to look ahead on your entrepreneurial journey and anticipate potential obstacles. The more you can foresee these hurdles, the more you can approach them with rational planning and proactive strategies, preventing those last-minute crises.

I've noticed that these emergencies often plague people who are constantly preoccupied with where the next cash infusion will come from. It's the entrepreneurial equivalent of living paycheck to paycheck, failing to save and plan. This self-perpetuating cycle of distraction and stress, where cash takes precedence over business strategy, hinders your ability to grow your business as you envision it.

While it might sound like an exaggeration, the reality is that every time you're forced to pause building your dream and divert your attention to address a cash emergency, your business is getting weaker. It's not just about the immediate cash problem—a failure to forecast cash flow is frequently the primary factor pulling you away from business development. It keeps you stuck in a rut.

Cash flow is simple to monitor. It's made up of "cash in" and "cash out." Here's a quick breakdown.

Cash In

Cash in tells you how much cash you're expecting in the door from sales. You have to be able to predict cash in at least a week out. If you can't, then it'll be a lot harder for you to conduct business with any confidence.

You can base your cash-in predictions on two things: outstanding invoices and averages for cash collected on jobs. The second option works best if you're a cash collection service company, like a plumber who goes to a job and gets paid on the spot.

If you have any cash coming in another way, whether you're putting money into the company, borrowing money, or getting funds through another means, include that in your cash-in calculations as well. Generally speaking, though, your cash-in number is cash from sales.

Cash Out

Cash out includes two main categories: expenses and debt service.

Expenses encompass materials, payroll, recurring subscription costs, and other charges slated for the upcoming week. In most cases, you can easily sort these expenses into the first and second weeks based on when they typically occur in the month. Creating a schedule to forecast your weekly cash outflows is a manageable task.

Debt service covers any loan payments and owner draws from the company.

Doing the Math

Once you've got your cash-in and cash-out numbers, you subtract one from the other and add the result to your bank balance. For example, if you start the week with $10,000 in the bank, and you anticipate an additional $5,000 in inflow and $7,000 in outflows, your week will close with $8,000 in the bank.

This approach provides you with a clear view of where you'll stand at the end of each week. Over time, as you build this habit, your forecasting skills will improve. You'll gain confidence in extending your predictions beyond a week, perhaps to the next month. With practice, you'll even project for the next quarter and year. Don't fret initially about absolute precision; you're nurturing the habit and strengthening your financial forecasting muscle.

Sales

When looking at sales as a measurement for efficiency, I recommend focusing on two areas: past recent sales and future projections.

First, examine sales that have already occurred, including those from last week. If your company handles invoicing separately from cash collections—particularly if you have accounts receivable or outstanding invoices awaiting payment—your weekly routine should include a thorough comparison between sales invoiced and sales collected in cash, since that's an easy place to leak money.

Second, review your accounts receivable to ensure timely follow-up on any overdue payments. If you're owed money, a delay in pursuing payment can lead to aging debts. By the time these outstanding payments come to your attention, it could be sixty or even ninety days overdue, significantly reducing the likelihood of collection. That's why you have to consistently and frequently review your accounts receivable and be quick to react when invoices haven't been paid.

When it comes to collecting payments on time, setting clear expectations with clients is vital. They need to understand that prompt payment is not only expected but essential. Tolerating late payments without repercussions can establish a precedent that leads to consistently delayed payments.

Remember, a sale isn't realized until you've received the cash. This concept is mission critical. One of the most necessary aspects of your weekly financial review is analyzing cash sales versus invoice sales.

Remember to take a look at that forecast. Look ahead at your sales pipeline. Evaluate the prospects you have for the upcoming week or month and assess the likelihood of these deals closing. Projecting these potential closures allows you to anticipate your sales for the coming period and figure out whether they align with your goals. If not, this early insight empowers you to do something to fix the situation.

The pipeline serves as a leading indicator, offering valuable insights into your future sales. This is where financial data proves its worth by helping you predict what lies ahead so that you can make informed decisions to shape the future instead of reacting to it as it unfolds.

The point here is to ask:

1. How much have we invoiced?
2. How much are we projected to invoice based on our pipeline?
3. Where does that place us concerning our target?

This leads us to the "go-get" figure. The rest of the month is composed of known invoices that are certain to occur. The "go-get" amount in this example stands at $89,000. Meanwhile, the pipeline suggests we have $145,000 in anticipated sales, indicating that we should be on track to meet our sales goal.

The go-get approach also allows us to detect any potential shortfall in advance, providing us with an opportunity to address it. The same applies to invoice sales, and this process extends to cash sales as well. This is the essence of sales analysis.

Expenses

Just like planning sales, it's a good idea to plan for expenses for the upcoming week. This doesn't have to be a formal budget; a budget sets an expectation. Most business owners set aside a budget for sales (which is really more of a goal for sales), and that's all they do. They don't think about expenses. They're not thinking, *If I sell this much, what will my expenses be for that?* Profit is whatever happens to be left over.

At the same time, the word "budget" scares a lot of people. They picture endless numbers, untold spreadsheets, and dizzying details. But if you think about a budget as a target, it feels more approachable. Most entrepreneurs have sales targets, and it's important to have expense targets, too, so that you know when you're spending more than you wanted.

Now you might ask, "Aren't reinvestments considered expenses?" Yes, they are. You have the flexibility to allocate funds within your business as you see fit, even if it means reinvesting extensively. This could imply increased spending in specific areas, but that's not necessarily a bad thing. The key is to be intentional about it. For instance, if you allocate funds for office chairs, ask yourself, "Will these chairs help my company make more money?" Or if you're contemplating investing in marketing or expanding your team, ask yourself,

"Will this help my business in the long run?" The idea is to plan ahead, measure your actions against your goals, and ensure you're moving in the right direction.

Customer Satisfaction

Customer satisfaction varies so widely between different service industries that it's challenging to pinpoint specific metrics. But once again, the idea here, in terms of efficiency, is to find leading indicators that inform you about potential troubles before they materialize into full-blown problems. Aim to identify the areas where customer satisfaction issues might arise for your business.

This process demands an understanding of the customer experience. Your customers are your customers because they expect value from your services. It's essential that you evaluate how satisfied they are with the value they received compared to what they expected. The sooner you can gather this information, the better. With the right metrics, potential customer turnover can be anticipated, and you can address it while you still have a chance to keep the customer.

As a business owner, you'll need to create your own approach to measuring customer satisfaction within your specific industry. In general, however, most entrepreneurs use some form of a customer survey. Do people actually complete customer satisfaction surveys? The answer is yes. Making it convenient for your customers is key. It should only take a minute or two and be a user-friendly experience.

Additionally, customers are more likely to participate when a business demonstrates a genuine interest in their opinions.

Surveys can work differently for different types of businesses. For instance, you might operate in a service-oriented business where employees develop some level of connection with customers. It doesn't have to be an intense, personal bond, but a relationship exists, nonetheless. Even if it's a technician visiting your home, a human interaction takes place. If that sounds like your business, you can incorporate a brief feedback mechanism into your payment process. This allows the customer to answer a few questions and, in seconds, provide valuable feedback.

For businesses offering ongoing services, like marketing agencies, you often have an account manager who maintains a relationship with the client. You can use this connection to your advantage by asking for feedback on the account manager, assuring the customer that their responses won't be linked back to them personally and emphasizing the importance of their input.

As you can see, solutions vary depending on your company's unique circumstances. However you're getting that data, though, you're transforming qualitative data into quantifiable metrics you can review weekly during your designated time. If you notice a decline in customer satisfaction, you can quickly identify and resolve the issue before it escalates. Waiting until unhappy customers start canceling services means you already have a significant problem on your hands.

An Efficient Business Is a Productive Business

I started riding motorcycles in my thirties, and I like to venture off-road. Through this, I've gleaned a lesson that applies not only to riding motorcycles but also to driving cars. This lesson is even more critical when navigating off-road terrain on two wheels, with bumps and rocks and all that jazz.

Instinct naturally directs your gaze to whatever is directly in front of you—in this case, the rocks and terrain under your motorcycle's front wheel. You have to consciously force yourself to lift your eyes and look farther ahead. Looking out helps you chart the course for where you're heading and, eventually, where you end up.

By the time you see the rock two feet in front of you, it's too late to do anything about it. You're in this spot—on the verge of disaster—because you weren't looking ahead.

The same principle applies to business. The further you can peer into the future, the better. It empowers you to avoid current issues and adopt a forward-looking mindset. You can navigate the upcoming week, month, or quarter with greater precision. You have to keep your eyes up and look ahead, and that's what this weekly dashboard routine forces you to do.

I have one client who unfortunately learned this lesson the hard way. Carmen's marketing agency was experiencing remarkable growth, jumping from under $100,000 a month to over $1 million a month in about a year, thanks to a couple of acquisitions. As you can imagine, this brought in a flurry of activities.

Carmen was keeping an eye on the top line, the sales figures, and cash flow, but she had a feeling something was off. She reached out to us, and we helped her look through the numbers with a weekly system of monitoring her financial dashboard. All of a sudden, a bunch of problems showed up. Customers weren't paying on time and the company was paying ad costs on behalf of customers who sometimes wouldn't pay for another sixty or ninety days. The business was floating costs and acting as a bank, minus the interest.

Carmen had to face a slew of unpleasant challenges, but this newfound perspective allowed her to tackle these issues head-on. A few months later, sales appeared to plateau, yet expenses were steadily climbing. Because she was diligently reviewing the numbers every week, Carmen promptly identified the situation and took swift action to control expenses. She engaged with the sales team to uncover the cause of the sales stagnation. No longer did she need to wait a month for the next financial report or wonder if it was merely a minor blip; she monitored the trend every week, then reacted quickly and corrected an issue before it turned into a bigger problem.

When I first started working with Carmen, her business was generating under $100,000 a month because a multitude of unnoticed problems were silently eroding her profits, akin to a leaky bucket—money flowed in, but it drained out faster than it could accumulate. Now, with revenues exceeding $1 million a month, she wields absolute command. A weekly report provides her with a precise understanding of the levers to pull, the conversations to initiate, and the actions to take before issues escalate into critical problems. Her business is far more organized and under control than it ever was at the under-a-hundred-thousand mark. The difference? Streamlining efficiency by consistently monitoring numbers that offer an objective reality—one that transcends human capacity to track on our own.

3

Accounting

When I started my first accounting job out of college, diploma still drying on the wall, my boss was explaining what she was expecting from me on a project she had assigned. She said something about the "PNL," an acronym that meant nothing to me. I nodded while she spoke, frantically thinking, *What's a PNL?* I finally had to ask her what she was talking about.

I'll never forget the look on her face. Turned out she had said "P&L"—referring to a profit and loss statement. She must have been thinking, *Oh my goodness. Who have we hired here?*

In school, we had only ever referred to financial statements in their full names—profit and loss statement (also called an income statement), balance sheet, statement of cash flows, what have you—in a formal, academic way.

Acronyms, shorthand jargon, real-life applications, using this knowledge to run a real business? It was all foreign to me. Even as an accounting graduate, I wasn't prepared for real-world business accounting. And if that was the case for someone who finished an undergraduate degree in accounting, what about everyone else? What about *you*?

Whether or not we go to school for it, in practical terms, we're not taught how to examine and understand financial statements. But it's so critical that we, as business owners, understand how to read and use these statements. They contain vital information that helps us make better decisions, recognize problems early on, and plan for consistent and profitable growth.

I'm an entrepreneur first and an accountant second, so I suffer from "shiny object disorder" as much as you do. I realize that nothing sounds more boring to most business owners than a discussion of financial statements. But think of these statements as an unbiased outside perspective of what's *really* happening in your business. Your financial statements tell you things you can't get from your intuition or your gut. They help you make more confident decisions, avoid mistakes, and give you the peace of mind and freedom to work on your business without the financial storms and uncertainty that drain the energy from so many of us.

If you want to think of it as eating your vegetables, that's fine. This is just one of those things that we, as entrepreneurs, need to learn and take ownership of so that we can lead our businesses and drive the results we want. That's what I want to teach you in this chapter.

I'm going to briefly cover some of the practical application accounting information I wish someone had bothered to teach me in college. The chapter is divided into three sections for the three main documents you need: the balance sheet, the profit and loss statement, and the statement of cash flows. By the end of this chapter, you should fully grasp how these documents can help you not only keep your business afloat, but also make great business decisions to help you achieve financial success.

Where You Are Now: The Balance Sheet

Unfortunately, the balance sheet is often, if not always, considered the most boring of the financial statements. It's the redheaded stepchild of financial statements, and it's the most ignored as a result. Many business owners, if they review financial statements at all, focus solely on the profit and loss statement. This is unfortunate, because when you look at a map, it's helpful to first figure out where you are. That's what the balance sheet does. It includes all kinds of details about the financial state of your business, usually at the end of a quarter or fiscal year.

To help you understand this concept, imagine two pictures. The first picture shows a dilapidated building on January 1, and the second picture shows a building all shiny and restored on December 31, after a full year. Each of those pictures represents a balance sheet, revealing in detail the state of your business at a fixed point in time.

If you were excited about the P&L, let's take a step back and look at the balance sheet first. Assuming the balance sheet is accurate, what should we be looking for? The balance sheet breaks down into three sections: assets, liabilities, and equity.

Assets

Assets can include current liquidity, inventory, accounts receivable, equipment—anything your business owns. This can be very eye-opening. By looking at your current liquidity on a balance sheet, you can gauge whether you have enough assets to cover short-term obligations like paychecks and utilities. Your balance sheet also dives into how efficiently you manage assets like inventory and accounts receivable. For example, if your accounts receivable are piling up, it might indicate that you need to tighten up your credit policies to improve cash flow.

On a balance sheet, assets are valuable items (either physical or digital) that either increase income or decrease expenses. Assets can include equipment, and this is an easy way to wrap your head around the concept. For instance, let's say someone purchases a machine. That machine may facilitate generating sales that wouldn't have been possible without it, thus boosting income. It may also enhance efficiency, allowing tasks to be completed more rapidly or proficiently than if done by an employee and thereby reducing expenses.

This principle applies even to simpler investments, like buying a computer for an employee. That computer enables the employee to work more efficiently and contribute to the company. It should, in theory, make the employee more effective.

That's the basis for analyzing your assets. To conduct this analysis, you need to examine all of them and ask yourself, "Are these assets performing?" or "Is every asset listed here either helping us increase sales or decrease expenses?"

Liabilities

A liability on a balance sheet is any amount you owe. It can include accounts payable, notes payable, and bank debt. The balance sheet also provides a glimpse of your long-term debt commitments. If you have, say, a substantial loan or mortgage, then your balance sheet will show you how this debt fits into your overall financial picture and whether it's manageable given your assets and equity.

As a rule, liability either increases an asset or decreases an expense. The above concept of purchasing a machine will help you understand this. Let's say you bought that expensive machine using a loan and will be paying in installments. You financed the equipment (computer) and therefore owe for it, but you would have the equipment recorded as the asset. You owe for that asset, but your liability helps to increase your assets. This is a standard debt scenario where the liability contributes to the asset.

Alternatively, you could refinance debt. This would enable you to lower the amount of interest that you're paying every month, which decreases expenses. You've taken on the liability of refinancing, but you've also wielded that liability to reduce costs.

Equity

Equity refers to the owner's investment in the company. At a simple level, equity is assets minus liabilities. For most small businesses, this is the net worth of the company. Equity growth over time is a sign of a healthy, profitable business, so pay attention to this.

The Two Big Balance Sheet Sins

You can probably tell now that your balance sheet equips you with indispensable financial information, complete with real numbers and examples. Using that information, you can make informed decisions and chart a successful course for your business. But there are two potentially catastrophic mistakes my clients make all the time with their balance sheets. I'll warn you about them here.

Ignoring the Balance Sheet

My client Carol has owned a successful landscaping business for several years. Near the end of the year, she came in to the office somewhat distraught. Her numbers weren't adding up; her P&L showed record profits, but the money wasn't in her accounts. She was nervous that someone was stealing from her. I asked her to hire an accountant before jumping to conclusions.

The next time I saw Carol, she said, "It was all a stupid mistake."

Carol had recorded sales on invoices that were due to her but hadn't been paid yet. These were listed on the accounts receivable line of her balance sheet, but Carol had failed to notice a huge number in her accounts receivable. Instead, when a payment came in against one of those invoices during a new month or quarter, she recorded that payment as a new sale instead of a payment against the open invoice. This essentially double counted the sale.

I knew exactly what had happened. "The payment was counted once on the invoice that was still open on the balance sheet," I said, "and a second time when the payment came in."

Carol shook her head in dismay. "We were counting the same sale twice—once on the invoice and then again when the cash was received. So my margins aren't nearly as good as I thought, but at least no one is stealing from me."

Carol could have avoided that whole situation if she had looked at her balance sheet. Many times, Carol overlooked the balance sheet—that redheaded stepchild of financial statements—and failed to take the time to review it. Carol is hardly my only client who has done this. I see it all the time. If the accounts receivable (a balance sheet account) are wrong, then something will definitely be wrong on the profit and loss statement. Many a business owner has glanced over that P&L and thought, *Hey, I'm doing pretty well.* Then it turns out they have $50,000 to $100,000 in sales that were double counted on the balance sheets upon which the P&L was based. This makes their whole assumption about their growth over a year false.

Not Crunching the Numbers Correctly

For the balance sheet to help you, it has to be correct. That might seem obvious, but many balance sheets are riddled with errors (remember, the balance sheet is often ignored). But getting the balance sheet right is fundamental in having accurate information on the profit and loss and the statement of cash flows. Mistakes on the balance sheet have cascading effects on the profit and loss statement as well as the statement of cash flows.

Take the example of Anders, the owner of a successful restaurant. Anders always reviewed his own finances, and one day he was excited to see that the balance sheet showed a substantial increase in accounts receivable. The increase seemed to indicate that the restaurant was doing better than ever, with customers apparently spending more.

Anders decided to make some moves. He hired more staff, ordered larger quantities of ingredients, and started planning some small renovations. The P&L also indicated strong revenue growth, so Anders felt sure his moves would pay off.

But what Anders didn't realize was that there was a mistake on the balance sheet, which meant the P&L was incorrect and falsely showing revenue growth. The increase in accounts receivable wasn't because of higher sales—it was an accounting error. The bookkeeper had mistakenly recorded some payments twice, inflating the figures on the balance sheet.

As months passed, Anders started to notice something was wrong. Customers weren't actually spending more; in fact, the restaurant's sales remained flat, and the additional staff and ingredients were eating into Anders's profits. Once the error was discovered, Anders was forced to cut back, shelve his planned renovations, and reevaluate.

I often see clients like this. They base their perception of their profit on the income statement, only to realize that their income statement is significantly inaccurate. This inaccuracy, when investigated, can usually be traced back to discrepancies on the balance sheet. As you can see, you can't look at the profit and loss statement by itself and assume that it's accurate. The balance sheet has to be accurate first since it serves as the foundation for reliable financial analysis.

How You Got Here: The Profit and Loss Statement

The second document I want to bring to your attention is the profit and loss statement, also known as an income statement. Business owners can't wait to get their hands on that P&L. The P&L is exciting because it tells the story of how your business did over a period of time. This financial report provides an overview of a company's revenues, costs, and expenses during a specific period (typically a month, quarter, or year). It gives business owners an idea of how things are going in the business and sheds light on aspects of the business that owners might not perceive from their day-to-day experience.

How is this different from the balance sheet? The profit and loss statement isn't like the wife and mother-in-law illusion. Instead, it's like a video that shows the story of how you moved from that dilapidated building to your newly restored building. The endpoints are your two balance sheets, but your P&L shows the in-between.

Here's the important part: If the ending pictures are wrong, it means that the story between those pictures will also be wrong. Let's say that ending photo, for example, was photoshopped to make the building look like it's in better shape than it really is. Your P&L tells the story of how you arrived at that (inaccurate) balance sheet. The story, by definition, is therefore also inaccurate. That's why both of these documents are so imperative for your business.

With an accurate P&L paired with accurate balance sheets, we can see the trends that reveal how your business has performed over time: sales trends, cost of materials and labor to deliver to customers, and overhead/administration costs. The P&L has the potential to bring factors within the business to the forefront—factors you might not recognize through your day-to-day involvement alone.

Elements of a Profit and Loss Statement

All the different elements in the profit and loss statement form the basis of income. That's why the P&L is sometimes referred to as the "income statement." The main categories listed on a P&L statement include:

Revenue or sales (total income generated from selling goods or services)
Less: Cost of goods sold, or COGS (direct costs related to producing or delivering what's sold)
Gross profit (revenue minus COGS, representing profit before operating expenses)
Less: Operating expenses (day-to-day costs, like salaries, rent, and marketing)
Operating income/profit (gross profit minus operating expenses)
Other income and expenses (nonoperating items, like interest or asset sales)
Income before taxes (profit before income tax is deducted)
Income tax expense (tax owed based on taxable income)
Net income/profit (final profit or loss after all expenses and taxes)

You may notice that you can divide this list into two broader categories: income and expenses. So let's talk about those two instead of delving in detail into all these little sections.

Income

There are various types of income that might flow into your business depending on the type of work you do. It can include income from selling goods or services and generating income from investments like rental properties. Wherever it comes from, the general purpose of income is to create cash flow. On your P&L, you can see exactly how much you've sold and how much you've received, which represents your gross income.

Remember that making a sale isn't the same as getting paid. The shorter the time you can turn a sale into cash flow, the better. You don't want accounts receivable piling up. Sometimes you have to deal with invoicing clients and then wait to get paid, but your objective with sales should always be to shorten that time. You want as little friction as possible between making a sale and receiving that cash. Ideally, every sale you make is immediately reflected in cash.

Expenses

The purpose of expenses is to create income. As you scrutinize the profit and loss statement, ask yourself if each expense is effectively creating income. Any expenses that aren't contributing to income should be cut out of your business.

On your P&L, you'll see two categories of expenses: COGS and overhead. COGS is any cost associated with the goods or services that were sold, while overhead is the general costs of keeping your business running (like payroll and keeping the lights on).

COGS is whatever cost you incur in order to deliver what someone is paying you to deliver. It's critical to measure that number, even though most business owners fail to do so. Being aware of your COGS allows you to break this general bucket of "expenses" into more actionable categories.

Alex, a client who runs a marketing agency, serves as a great example. His sales were going up every month, but he wasn't making money. His P&L showed losses month after month.

"I don't understand why," he told me. "Sales are going up! How is this happening?"

"Let's take a look at your P&L," I said. "We'll figure this out."

I wasn't surprised to find his profit and loss was a mess. Everything was scattered around. Like a lot of business owners, Alex was only thinking about sales. Believing that you have to get more and more sales to make money, he wasn't looking at the whole P&L.

Alex's profit and loss statement failed to distinguish between cost of sales and overhead costs. After we did some organizing and differentiated between overhead costs and customer-delivery-related costs, the problem revealed itself. Alex's gross margins on delivering the goods didn't leave room for him to cover general expenses, including overhead expenses. The problem wasn't about keeping the lights on in the building or paying administrative personnel and similar costs; the problem was the cost of sales.

"Okay," he finally said, sighing. "I have too many people on my delivery team."

"Yes," I said.

"They're taking too long to complete projects."

"Definitely."

"I have to lay some of them off." He ran his hand down his face.

"It won't be fun," I said. "But with your sales as good as they are, once you fix up your operating costs, your business will be thriving. You can take better care of your employees and even scale up the right way over time."

Alex did what he had to do. As soon as he reduced his COGS, his strong sales numbers buoyed his business the way he had intended. His P&L is now spotless, and he refers to it often.

Let's talk about operating costs—your mortgage or rent, office equipment, and the like. When paying for those, you still have to ask yourself, "How effectively is this creating income?" A good practical example of this is sales and marketing activities that don't create extra income, like untargeted general advertising. These can also be operating expenses you shoulder because they're fun, nice, or give you a sense of luxury, like a fancy office, premium desks, and catered lunches. But is that creating extra income?

Sometimes the answer may be yes, but it depends on whether customers see or appreciate these activities. Springing for a modern desk in your front-facing office where you meet with clients is very different from shelling out big bucks for bespoke desks for the entire marketing team. I mostly work from home, and I bought myself a mid-grade standup desk that's better for my physical health. That pays off in the long run, but what I didn't do is spend a ton of money on a mahogany, godfather-style desk when nobody other than my family is going to see it.

Back before I started my first business, I worked for a major multinational aerospace company. The chief financial officer (CFO) and I were talking about overhead expenses, and he said in his thick Dutch accent, "We have to be ruthless about looking at overhead expenses. They are like body fat: Once you get it, it's extremely hard to get rid of."

That stuck with me. Business owners need to be careful about any kind of overhead they add. It's too easy to accumulate those kinds of non-client expenses or not-directly-related-to-client expenses. Those tend to become significant and often end up sinking companies, as owners get accustomed to spending a lot of money on things that don't increase income.

As you can see, the balance sheet and P&L are both significant, but they aren't the only reports you'll need to pay attention to. Next, I want to discuss another statement that business owners tend to ignore: the statement of cash flows.

Cash Is King: The Statement of Cash Flows

The third and final accounting document you must pay attention to as a business owner is the statement of cash flows. This document helps you connect the dots between your P&L and what's in your bank account. It's a financial statement that reconciles your profit or loss with the dollar amount in your account. It starts with the net income from the profit and loss statement, then adds back non-cash expenses, such as depreciation and amortization. Finally, it subtracts out non-cash revenues, such as gains on the sale of assets. In the end, it shows you exactly where your business stands financially.

The statement of cash flows is significant because profit doesn't always equal cash flow. Often, business owners look at their profit and loss statement and see either a profit or a loss. They then assume that their profit is their cash flow, but that's not the case (remember Anders and his restaurant?). A company can easily make a profit but still have a negative cash flow if it had to spend a lot of money on inventory or accounts receivable.

Your statement of cash flows begins with net income as the top item. So if your net income was $50,000, the first line on the statement will also be $50,000. Then, to help you figure out what's going on, the statement of cash flows breaks down your cash into three categories: operating cash flow, investing cash flow, and financing cash flow. Wondering what that means? I've got you covered.

Cash Flow from Operations

Operating cash flow comes first on your statement of cash flows. It shows the cash generated from the company's core business activities, such as selling goods and services. From there, cash flow operations run through all the factors that affected cash that were not necessarily on the profit and loss statement.

A common example of this is accounts receivable, which we discussed in the previous section. Let's say you invoiced $20,000 but that client hasn't paid you yet. Your profit and loss statement shows that $100,000 in sales were invoiced that month, but $20,000 of that amount hasn't been received in that month.

Your statement of cash flows would start out with the initial $50,000 in profit. You would then subtract the $20,000 that you didn't collect. Consequently, the net cash from operations is $30,000, not the original $50,000. There might be other items as well. For instance, you may have expenses that you paid with a credit card but haven't paid the bill for yet. In this situation, you recorded the expense, but the cash hasn't left your account yet due to the typical thirty-day credit card payment period.

Cash Flow from Investing

The second part of the statement of cash flows is cash from investing, which pertains to the buying and selling of assets such as land, buildings, and equipment. Let's say you purchased two new computers last month for $5,000. These computers are assets, so they're reflected on the balance sheet rather than the profit and loss statement. As a result, they aren't recorded as expenses on the P&L, but you did spend that money. This accounts for another $5,000 in negative cash flow from investing.

Cash Flow from Financing

The third category is cash flow from financing, which involves activities like borrowing money or repaying debts. For instance, let's say you loaned your business $30,000. You turned a profit and have the money to make a payment, so the company makes a loan payment of $30,000 back to you. Your statement of cash flows shows this cash flow from financing.

Let's follow our statement of cash flows:

- The profit and loss statement claimed $50,000 in profit.
- Only $30,000 was cash flow profit from operations because some of the invoices weren't collected.
- Another $5,000 went to the computers; the business is now down to $25,000 in cash.
- The business paid $30,000 on the loan in the financing section.

After looking at that statement of cash flows, it makes sense that the bank account went down by $5,000, even though the business saw $50,000 in profit.

Keeping Accountable

Far too many business owners don't understand their financial statements or even look at them. Instead, they assign that responsibility to their bookkeeper or accountant. They like to tell me they would "rather not think about it" and "rather not look at it." They consider financial statements boring, merely a reflection of the stuff that already happened. They want to keep marching forward, and as a result, business owners often perceive financial statements as only useful for sending historical data to a bank or for filing tax returns. If you think like that, you're willingly putting blinders on.

Most business owners may not prepare their own financial statements, but they're certainly responsible for them. Responsibility means reviewing them and being able to understand them.

Here's what it comes down to: Nobody, not your accountant or bookkeeper, should be as intimately familiar with your actual operations and transactions as you. Nobody cares as much about those numbers as you because it's not their business—it's yours.

You have to step up and make time to review those numbers. These statements may not have amazing entertainment value, but they do offer critical information about your present financial standing and how you got to where you are today. Keep up with your balance sheet, P&L, and statement of cash flows, and you'll have all the key information you need to make good decisions.

4

Leverage

One summer I was getting help installing a massive above-ground pool in my back yard. We had filled it halfway with water when we noticed some of the legs weren't straight. At this point, with gallons and gallons of water in the pool, it weighed thousands of pounds. There was no way we could move it, but we also didn't want to drain it.

The solution? We set up a sturdy pole as a lever, which allowed us to lift this monstrosity without exerting too much energy. The leverage made the heavy lift easier. Leverage can do the same for your business. Except instead of a pole, you'll be leveraging three main assets: money, time, and expertise. And you won't be leveraging your own assets—you'll be leveraging other people's money, time, and expertise to help you achieve your business goals. Here's how it works.

Money

When it comes to leveraging money, I'm not talking about draining your bank accounts into your business. Instead, it's best to leverage other people's money. This can come in multiple forms, but the most common one is debt.

Debt breaks down into two different kinds: personal debt and investment debt. Let's take a closer look at each.

Personal Debt

Personal debt includes anything that doesn't actively produce income in your life. That may include a car loan, mortgage, credit card debt, and the like. Personal debt is generally negative, as it slows down your path to financial freedom.

People often confuse personal debt and investment debt. For example, you may consider a house an investment. That's true in a sense, but a personal residence doesn't produce income, and a house isn't an investment if it doesn't produce income. Sure, it's an asset that goes up in value, and when and if you do eventually sell, you may make a profit. Until that time, however, I wouldn't consider your house an investment unless you're a house flipper who moves every few years. The house just sits there, a part of your lifestyle not actively producing income, so I wouldn't categorize it as investment debt. It falls under personal debt.

As a general rule, you want to minimize and pay down personal debt as quickly as you can. I'm not a hardliner on personal debt because personal debt sometimes enables you to do other things. For instance, as an entrepreneur, you might take out a second mortgage on your home to open a business. Even though it's a second mortgage on your home, it's going toward an income-producing asset. At that point, rather than personal debt, we'd be dealing with investment debt.

Investment Debt

Investment debt is for income-producing assets that allow you to accelerate your overall income and wealth generation. Unlike personal debt, these assets typically cover the debt and generate additional income. When done correctly, the assets not only pay for the debt but also yield profits.

Here's a good example. I had a client named Jake, a therapist who wanted to open his own practice. He had a wife, kids, and a mortgage, so he needed to bring in income. He and his wife didn't have enough savings, so there were two possible routes he could have taken.

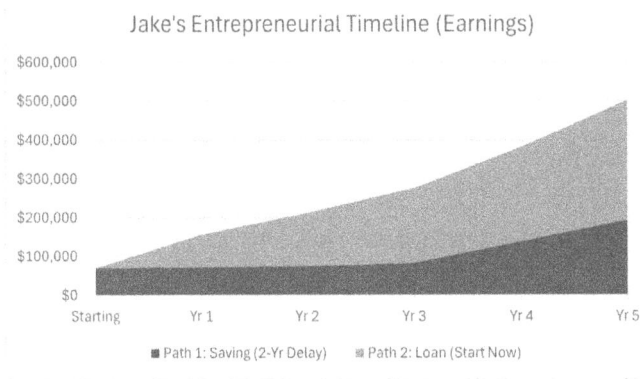

Jake's Entrepreneurial Timeline (Earnings)

Jake could have tried to save until he had a year's worth of savings to cover him while he got started on his practice. It probably would have taken him two years to save up that amount of money on his annual salary of $70,000. To speed things up, after consulting with me, Jake took out a second mortgage on his home to start his practice. Within a year, he was making more than his salary, and within two years, he was probably making double.

As you can see from these graphs, if you can speed up your timeline at the expense of personal debt, then those results get amplified as you project into the future a couple of years. In Jake's case, even though the debt was on his house, it can technically be considered investment debt.

A word of caution. When you finance a purchase— whether it's real estate or a business (using a small business administration loan for business or taking out a mortgage on real estate, for example)—it can be easy to borrow a substantial amount of money. This enables you to move faster, which is both a positive and a negative. Often, people make larger decisions more rapidly when they have access to financing. If things go wrong, you end up with quicksand.

Generally, when you're financing something, you put down only a relatively small percentage. In the case of real estate, you put down between 20 to 25 percent. If you're buying a business, it's generally similar in that regard. Your "skin in the game" is smaller, which can make it emotionally easier to make significant decisions or become numb to them. The money isn't directly coming out of your bank account, so who cares, right? This can lead to people making decisions without being careful.

I had a client named Jan who was a successful entrepreneur in the manufacturing sector. She used debt to finance the purchase of a second manufacturing business and was hooked, becoming extremely focused on growing through this acquisition model. Because she was using debt, making these decisions became easy for her. Unfortunately, it backfired.

Over a relatively short period, Jan purchased several other manufacturing businesses in her industry, making four acquisitions within two years. She financed it all with debt. The acquisitions weren't disasters, but they turned out to be fairly mediocre, with some barely covering the debt and others not even managing to break even.

Jan ended up with a debt of around $3 million with a relatively high interest rate. Each month she had to shell out $180,000 in loan repayments. So before making any cash profit, she had to cover $180,000 of debt on top of her operating expenses. It was a bad situation, and we got her out of it, but it wasn't fun.

As you can see, investment debt works great in theory: borrow money to make money. But in practice, it can be too easy to overestimate how well an asset will perform. When debt amplifies and hastens your decisions, you can get yourself into a lot of trouble and find yourself in a difficult situation.

I can't deny that investment debt helps you go faster, in the right circumstances. Jake is just one positive example. I could cite example after example of clients who used debt to purchase income-producing assets, thereby significantly speeding up their profit creation timeline. Sometimes they sped up their timeline by a factor of five or more. When used correctly, investment debt acts as fuel on a fire and can lead to substantial growth. It can be beneficial, but at the same time, we all make mistakes in business. You better be sure about what you're doing before you pull the trigger.

Don't use debt until you're confident in your plan.

Cash Injection

There's one more scenario to consider here—the cash injection. Whether it's an inheritance, an insurance payout, a severance package, or a lottery win, people sometimes come into unexpected money. Even if it isn't a huge amount, you can use these funds to avoid borrowing and start or build your business without any debt at all.

I started my business as a side hustle in 2010 while working for a traditional employer. In 2015, another company that already had a finance department acquired the company I worked for. They didn't need to keep me, and they gave me some severance money. That was enough to give me the flexibility to go full time on my own without having to take on debt.

It wasn't a lot of money. I think I received $20,000, which may sound like a lot, but it's only a couple of months' worth when you have a family, a mortgage, and expenses. It was tight, and I made so many mistakes over those first few years, but I still managed to grow my business.

If I had debt, things might have been different. First, I wouldn't have felt as desperate or under as much pressure. I'm not sure that would have been a good thing. It was probably good for me to feel all that pressure and have to push myself during those first years. Second, I probably would have spent the money on things that I hoped would make life easier. I might have made a bad hire and invested in areas like sales and marketing, which I didn't know much about at that point. This could have potentially wasted resources in the wrong areas.

I can't definitively say whether it would have been better or worse, but what I can say is that I was able to start my accounting firm with no debt, thanks to that severance package. I'm glad I did because it made me more cautious in my decision-making, and it kept me hungry and under pressure, which was probably a good thing.

I started my firm full time by the end of 2015 and sold it for seven figures in 2021, all without taking on debt. I don't regret avoiding the use of other people's money, and it's certainly achievable. So if you find yourself with some extra funds at some point, consider using them to give your business a boost and speed up that timeline.

Time

My client Will owns a marketing agency. Terrible at delegating, he was constantly stuck doing all sorts of trivial tasks. He never seemed to have any time, even from our perspective. When we sent him emails, he took forever to respond, then only answered one of the four things we asked. It was obvious that things were falling through the cracks. Unsurprisingly, under the circumstances, his business was unable to grow and remained maxed out at about $500,000 in revenue per year.

Suddenly, Will's business started to take off. In one year, his agency went from being capped at revenues of $500,000 to revenues of $800,000 the next year, then $1.2 million the year after that, and finally $3 million the year after that. He also became much better at answering his emails. When I finally got Will into my office, I asked him about the sudden growth.

"It all started when I came across Gino Wickman's fantastic book *Traction*," he told me. "You should check it out. It's what got me on the right track. They have this whole system called the EOS."

"EOS?" I asked.

"Entrepreneurial Operating System," Will said. "It provided me with a framework to start building a team and delegating core functions to them. I realized that my sales needed a boost, but I thought I was the only one who could sell my product effectively. I was wrong."

I nodded. "Delegating sales can be tough. What did you do?"

"I hired a salesperson already experienced in the industry and let them take over. Our sales took off! At that point, I had to delegate other operational tasks, but I felt a little more comfortable with the whole idea."

"So you're delegating a lot now?"

"I'm at a point where I own the agency but only deal with it a couple of hours a week," Will said. "I have a few meetings with my leadership team, and that's it."

One of the things I love about owning a business is that it forces us to develop in so many different areas, especially at the beginning. The danger, however, is that because so many different things need to be done, you might try to do everything yourself. I'm guilty of it; Will was guilty of it. Practically every entrepreneur is. But the truth is that other people's time is non-negotiable for business owners. You have to delegate tasks that aren't essential to your success.

Most entrepreneurs never cross the million-dollar sales threshold—they never even think of crossing it, and one key reason is the lack of delegation. Many, many entrepreneurs successfully run their businesses, and they aren't going out of business. But they're not free from their businesses, and these businesses have caps. The entrepreneur acts as the bottleneck because everything has to go through them. Their time becomes the bottleneck.

Whether past negative experiences or fear of taking that step holds them back, these folks never cross the threshold to delegate and take advantage of other people's time to allow the business to grow. This becomes the major chokepoint for entrepreneurs on the road to financial freedom, whether they intend to eventually sell their business or continue owning it without it owning them or their time. In either case, the degree of their success comes down to how effectively they delegate.

Don't Wait, Delegate

There are two ways entrepreneurs tend to mess up when it comes to delegation. The first is refusing to let go of anything. It can be scary at first, but as business owners, we need to continually audit what we do. Ask yourself, "Which of these things are least helpful in getting me to where I want to go in my business and life?" You don't need to take out the trash; you don't need to answer every email personally; you don't need to pay the utility bill. You can find someone to take care of these tasks so you can focus on the important ones.

The counterexample is when you delegate something and entirely wash your hands of it. You have to be intentional and careful about eliminating the lowest-value tasks, and when you find someone to do these things for you, you need to find a way to manage them effectively. This becomes especially problematic when you're delegating something you don't fully understand because you then have no control over the result.

A classic example of this is accounting. So many business owners don't want to deal with taxes at all because they have so many things going on. They hand over everything to their accountant and are happy to be rid of it. They don't think through questions like, "How will I ensure the accountant is doing a good job?" or "How do I hold the accountant accountable?" We often assume that when hiring someone, they will solve the problem for us, but that's not always the case.

More often than not, when we delegate as business owners, we're delegating a specific role (like that of the accountant). If you don't know how to manage that delegation process, then it's pure luck if you get good results, and you usually won't be that fortunate. Then people wonder why they feel like their accountant isn't providing them with good tax strategies, why their accountant never thinks about them unless they're talking to them, and why they're getting mediocre results. They're frustrated with the results but haven't realized that it's because their delegation is ineffective. We'll discuss this in more detail in chapter 6.

Expertise

When I first started my firm, I didn't know how to get clients, and it was holding me back. I had a website, and I might have had some paid search ads on Google, but I wasn't getting clients with any sort of consistency. I saw an advertisement for a coach who helped accountants start and grow their firms. His main focus was explaining how to market and generate leads, then progress to selling and closing deals at higher values.

The coach charged $6,000 for his training, which took place over a year or so. Choosing to buy his services was probably the scariest decision I've ever made. Obviously, I've made much larger financial decisions since then, but none scarier than what that $6,000 meant to me at the time. My severance was dwindling, and I was dipping into my savings every month. I was already earning some money from the firm, but the idea of taking $6,000, a third or a fourth of my savings, and investing it in this coach was terrifying. If it didn't work, it would be extremely painful.

Before that point, I hadn't invested in myself, besides higher education. I didn't understand that improving myself could lead to making a lot more money. That decision represented a turning point in my attitude toward self-investment, and it turned out to be one of the best decisions I've ever made.

That coach taught me how to market my firm and make sales with clients. I didn't even agree with everything he said or taught, but I unquestionably made that investment in training. It's hard to put a value on what my return on that investment was, and that has been the case over and over again.

Leveraging other people's expertise is about acquiring knowledge. To leverage other people's knowledge effectively, you need to consider how you can obtain that knowledge in a way that facilitates implementation. How can you leverage others' knowledge in a way that helps you implement it and make changes? Generally, this comes down to how invested you are in acquiring that knowledge, which is often tied to time and money.

I've paid and traveled to attend conferences and seminars on tax strategies that either presented information I already knew or were full of gimmicky strategies I wanted to avoid. But even at those conferences, where 90 percent of the information was useless to me, I got 10 percent useful information. If I picked up just one thing, one new piece of knowledge, and then implemented it, attending the conference was worth it. Do that, and you'll almost never spend money to acquire knowledge from other people and not have it be a good investment.

The caveat here is that you must take action and implement what you've learned. I might have listened to something hundreds of times on a podcast or an audiobook and thought it was terrific. But if I don't do anything with it immediately, an hour later it's gone—poof. But if I go to a conference, I'm physically traveling somewhere, sitting in a room with my phone off, paying attention, and I've paid money for it. I'm invested in the outcome—I have skin in the game—making me more likely to implement that knowledge immediately after.

However you get your expertise, the key here is that you can progress much faster if you accept that there's a lot you don't know and that others are better at certain things than you are. If you can learn from others and improve yourself, you remove constraints that hinder you from making more money. This is almost always a good investment, as long as you promptly focus on implementing what you've learned.

Resources for Gaining Expertise

You can get information—coaching, seminars, and the like—from many different places, but Alex Hormozi, a prominent figure in entrepreneurship, sheds insight on how you should go about gaining expertise.

In a thought-provoking YouTube video, Hormozi shared the perspective that "you get more out of reading one book that is great five times than out of reading five mediocre books."[4] Mastering the principles from a single source through repeated study and diligent implementation is better than reaching for everything you can find and failing to act.

Books

The good thing about books is that you can acquire a lot of information from them inexpensively, making them a fantastic starting point. The main focus, however, should always be on implementation rather than merely consuming the material. As an entrepreneur, hopefully you're already good at implementation. So if you can read a book and

---

4   Alex Hormozi, "Read 1 Good Book 5 Times," YouTube video, 0:24, June 25, 2023, https://www.youtube.com/watch?v=8J881zhJsp4.

take its advice (like you hopefully are with this one), by all means do so.

Seminars

If you're weak in a particular area, you can probably find a seminar for it. I understand it can be a hassle to travel; I don't particularly enjoy it myself. But attend the seminar. You might talk yourself into attending it online, thinking, *I'll just watch it from here. Same information.* In my experience, it doesn't hit the same. When you're on your computer, you might receive an email or chat with a team member. Your spouse may poke their head into your office and ask you to pick up the kids from school.

Whatever it is, distractions pop up, and you don't have the same level of engagement as when you get on a plane, go to the event, and physically sit in the room. You might even go in with the expectation that this is all a waste of time, but you're looking for that one thing you can take and implement. If you do that, it's hard to spend money poorly on things that provide knowledge in areas where you're weak.

Networking Events

Some people might argue against networking, and I admit I wasn't initially convinced of its value either. I tend to be quite antisocial and not much of a talker, but now that I think about it, I've made a few contacts that have proven beneficial. If you go to a networking event in person, whether local or regional or tied to a conference, you're more likely to reap the benefits and get some value out of it.

Coaches

In 2020, when I was thirty-five, I threw my back out. It was awful. I thought, *Oh boy, this can't happen twice a year, or even once a year. This can't be the norm for me for the next several decades.*

Even though I had a gym membership, it was pandemic times, and I couldn't use it. I had tried the workout-at-home routine in the morning, but with no accountability, I wasn't able to stay consistent. The lack of a good plan, a lack of knowledge about how to work out the right way without injury, and a lack of accountability meant that I never worked out, and my back paid the price.

I was desperate. I reached out to a personal trainer who ran a small gym and signed up for a package. If I didn't go on a day I said I would, the trainer texted me. He helped me work through my back injury and build up some structural muscle, and I haven't thrown out my back since.

Why does this anecdote fall under coaches? Well, a coach is a personal trainer for your brain. You buy in, you're invested, and coaches keep you accountable. They teach you new skills and check up on you. They don't disappear after you turn the last page or after the weekend—they're there for as long as you need them, forcing you to be consistent. That's why coaches, despite the cost, have worked well for me and will likely work well for you.

Courses

I realize the irony of writing this in my own book, but books are often purchased without implementing the content. Courses and coaching tend to be popular because they require us to put more money and time into their process. Like a coach, a paid course, whether online or in person, may include action steps to ensure that we implement the knowledge. This leads to results that justify the investment of time and money. Because we've invested more time and more money in courses, we're compelled to implement that knowledge immediately.

Leverage Yourself to Success

It took me eleven years from start to finish between beginning my side hustle in 2010 to selling my business in 2021. Plotted on a graph, those eleven years show a relatively flat line extending for the first five or six years, then it starts to go up when I got that cash injection, and then the line curves exponentially at the point of selling.

Now, compare that with what happened after I sold that firm and started taking on a handful of clients. My new business grew so quickly that it felt effortless. It wasn't even a deliberate attempt to grow; it was about helping someone I knew, and it naturally and smoothly expanded. Within two years, I had a firm generating the same revenue as before. What took me eleven years the first time, took just two years the second time.

What happened? First, I had more money to invest, not necessarily from leveraging other people's money but because I had proceeds from the sale. I therefore invested more quickly and brought in a team that could assist me and alleviate some of the burden on my time. Collectively, we accomplished more, and my ability to hire and delegate improved.

Second, I had all the knowledge and expertise I gained from that decade to get me to where I was. With that proper leveraging of money, time, and expertise, I almost casually strolled into the same-size business that I had before, built in one-fifth the time. That's the power of leverage.

I'm far from perfect, of course, and I certainly don't have it all figured out. I'm aware that for me to scale, for me to take my business and my life to where I want it to go over the next five to ten years, I have a whole bunch more leveraging to do. At some point, I probably need to look at leveraging other people's money. I need to get better at leveraging other people's time and better at building a team. I still have a ton of expertise that I need to acquire. With more leverage, who knows where I'll end up.

The point is, the tools and resources we leverage allow us to move forward faster. If you're considering how to speed up your process, you should think carefully and use leverage judiciously. It's like gasoline on a fire, which can be either advantageous or detrimental, depending on how you control it. But generally speaking, if you're stuck or things are progressing slower than you want, then you should ask yourself which area you're weak in. Could you progress faster if you got a little boost?

5

Tax Strategy

In the previous chapters, we've discussed managing cash flow and understanding how to use your financial statements to control your business. Here, we'll focus on the tax side.

Over the last twelve years, I've helped my clients save over $10 million in taxes and assisted dozens of entrepreneurs in progressing from zero to millionaires in less than a decade. When I sold my chartered professional accounting firm in 2021, I shifted my focus to bringing this knowledge to entrepreneurs who are perhaps earlier than I am in their journeys.

Taxes can go two ways for business owners. On the negative side, you can end up overpaying by a lot. On the positive side, your business can provide tax incentives for investors and yourself to advance everyone's financial freedom. This is a seemingly straightforward step, but it's often the most overlooked and underserved aspect for entrepreneurs. Many business owners find themselves stuck, merely filing tax returns without strategic tax advice from their accountants.

If you've made previous attempts to minimize your taxes and failed to do so, I want to assure you that it's not your fault. So much information exists out there that trying to take it in can feel like drinking from a fire hose. It can leave you overwhelmed, spinning in circles, and unsure of what or whom to trust. This information overload can stop you from making progress and hitting your goals.

So if you've ever felt that you aren't cut out for this or can't achieve success through your business, I want to alleviate those fears. You need the right model to follow, unlocking the cash flow and wealth readily available to us as business owners.

I wrote this chapter with two different groups of people in mind. One, if you're an entrepreneur earning less than $350,000 annually, I want to give you a new tax model. This model will enable you to eliminate cash flow concerns and reach seven-figure profits three to four times faster than conventional wisdom suggests is possible.

Two, for those of you earning more than $350,000 annually, I want to provide you with a strategy to scale your business to $1 million and beyond. This involves identifying and addressing areas where your business might be leaking money due to inefficiencies or unnecessary expenses. When you operate at this level, these savings add up quickly.

My message to you is this, regardless of which camp you fall into: The key to tax strategy—and bottom-line profits—is to examine financial metrics, anticipate future challenges, and create a plan to identify and overcome obstacles.

The Real Cost of Poor Tax Strategy

After-Tax Earnings With and Without Tax Planning

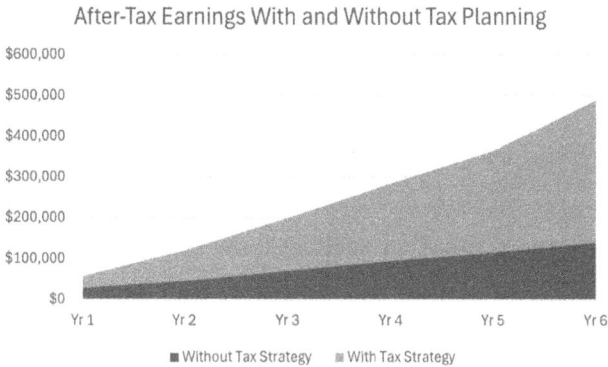

■ Without Tax Strategy   ■ With Tax Strategy

To kick things off, consider two hypothetical businesses. In the first year, both businesses generate $30,000 in profit. One of them doesn't have good tax planning, though, and ends up overpaying by $2,500. The other has a good tax plan, keeps the $2,500, and wisely reinvests it in marketing.

Already there's a difference between the two businesses. The one that reinvested in marketing has an advantage going into that second year. Over time, this starts to make a profound difference. During year two, the first business may continue to overpay taxes, while the second business saves and reinvests $5,000. The two companies will soon see increasingly divergent paths. Much like a shift in train tracks can lead to trains ending up miles or even hundreds of miles apart, one of these businesses has a clear path to success, while the other one's fate isn't as clear.

My client Tina is a great example. Tina thought she was doing everything right. As an influencer, she was starting to make six figures. Her business was growing steadily, and when she had her chartered professional account (CPA) prepare her return, she assumed everything was in order. Then, abruptly, she got hit with an audit. The IRS demanded another $40,000 from her, and she came to us for help.

Upon reviewing her return, I realized she had classified many expenses as meals and entertainment. All those classifications posed an audit risk and raised a red flag for the IRS. That resulted in a slew of new problems. The IRS wanted to see receipts for all her expenses—a colossal nightmare. It drained her energy and threw a significant hurdle in her path.

Tina's woes didn't end with her classifications. Upon examining her tax return, not only did I discover a glaring red flag that would have been easily preventable with strategic planning, but I also found that she hadn't established the right entity structure. Consequently, she overpaid by $10,000 compared to what a more informed approach to entity structures could have saved her. Luckily, I was able to help Tina structure her business and strategize to stop the cycle and allow her business to thrive.

For a new or growing business, this is the kind of obstacle that holds you back for a year or two as you overpay taxes, grapple with audits, and strive to avoid giving $40,000 to the IRS. A business without these problems may not feel like it's doing anything special, but the lack of the obstacle allows it to move forward. That's why tax strategy is so essential from the beginning.

The Foundation: Getting Proactive

According to a study by the Treasury Inspector General for Tax Administration, the average entrepreneur overpays taxes by $11,638 every year.[5] Many entrepreneurs surpass this number. Imagine the cumulative effect of that amount, year after year. It's worth emphasizing—this isn't a little bit of money. Stack it up over time and think of what you could achieve.

That's why you have to be proactive about keeping that money. Rather than viewing taxes solely as an expense, consider how you can leverage existing incentives to help you not only save money but accelerate your overall timeline toward success. With that in mind, in this section, we'll explore three key strategies you can use to reduce your tax burden.

---

5   "Study Shows Small Companies May Have Overpaid Taxes," GovCon, n.d., https://www.govcon.com/doc/study-shows-small-companies-may-have-overpaid-0001.

Examine Your Situation

The first step toward a proactive tax strategy is awareness. You have to examine and comprehend your tax obligations. Remember, you can delegate the execution to someone else, but you must be the mastermind behind your financial strategy. No one will ever have the same level of commitment or understanding of your situation as you do. You are the linchpin in this process. For your designated professional to deliver the results you want, you have to know what you want.

View your CPA as a resource, not the full owner of your tax burden, even if you're paying them a significant fee. Be actively engaged in and in control of your financial decisions, as I've said in previous chapters. No one cares about your money more than you do!

Almost no entrepreneur automatically examines their tax situation as much as they need to. To do that, though, you have to understand your situation, which means you have a specific kind of relationship with your CPA.

Hire an Actual CPA, Not Just a Tax Person

Many entrepreneurs don't have an explicitly defined relationship with their CPA. You may be working with one of two different types of accountants. Some accountants have a small number of clients, and each of those clients pays them a substantial amount of money. These CPAs think proactively, providing specific insights about your situation. On the other hand, there are accountants whose many

clients pay less for a lesser product: the simple preparation
of a tax return.

Despite the huge difference in the depth of service, the
difference between CPAs and tax-preparation accountants
isn't usually clear at first. This can be tricky for entrepreneurs to understand, especially with the higher price tag for
a CPA. Moreover, new entrepreneurs might not be able to
afford to pay a large amount. So these simple tax-prep folks
get flooded with clients and have less time to spend with
each client.

At my first business, I had a lot of people bring me on
to be a simple tax preparer, paying a low fee. They would
then reach out to me in July, saying, "What can I do to minimize my taxes this year? I've earned a bit more money, and
I'm concerned." My initial thoughts and what I'd like to say?
"You hired me to prepare a tax return, and I have a long list
of other tax returns to deal with. How can I invest half a day
or a full day examining your specific situation?"

At some point, the light bulb went on, and I realized
that my firm needed to focus on tax strategy. We shifted our
business model and our prices went up, but our service is
also so much more valuable. The tax return went to the end
of the process, merely documenting what we had already
meticulously planned out.

After we made that change, I found myself in recurring
conversations with entrepreneurs who couldn't afford our
services, which at that point was primarily focused on stra-

tegic consulting. There was no suitable alternative I could recommend to them. Unfortunately, the only option was to turn to basic tax-prep folks for basic tax-return preparation, which wasn't an ideal solution. And that's precisely why I founded Contigo Advisors—to give entrepreneurs a middle ground.

I want to emphasize that this isn't a sales pitch. Rather, I want to show you that hiring a basic tax preparer isn't enough. If you want to proactively manage your tax burden, you need a solid understanding of your finances so you can hold your accountant accountable. If you're not a financial expert yourself, a real CPA empowers you to understand your tax strategy.

Study Your Current and Projected Taxes

Once you have a good understanding of your situation, it's time to create a basic tax projection, which can lead to broader financial projections. It doesn't have to be overly complex; instead, consider how much profit you anticipate making this year and how it will impact your tax return. You now have a starting point for identifying potential areas of concern. By gaining insight into what your tax return will likely look like next April, you can take proactive measures while there's still time.

Put Your Taxes into a Scorecard

To take your understanding of your taxes further, create a scorecard using your current taxes and projected future taxes to assess your tax projection from various angles. It's essential to evaluate your situation across different metrics to understand what's going on. The following four areas should make it onto your scorecard:

Effective tax rate: Are you shelling out 37 percent on every additional dollar you earn? That's far from ideal and demands action.

Earnings before interest, taxes, depreciation, and appreciation (EBITDA): EBITDA might sound like a complex accounting term, but it's essentially your gross earnings before accounting for depreciation or employing any tax-optimization strategies. This metric allows you to gauge how much tax you're paying relative to your gross earnings. Monitoring this year over year can provide insights into whether you're paying more or less in taxes on each earned dollar compared to the previous year.

Qualified business income (QBI): QBI is an often-overlooked aspect that comes with a substantial 20 percent deduction opportunity for those who qualify. Eligibility can vary, however, depending on your situation. Many business owners miss the chance to plan for this deduction, only to discover their eligibility when filing taxes. Have this on your scorecard early enough, and you can reorganize your circumstances to ensure you qualify, thereby seizing this valuable opportunity while there's still time.

Pretax and posttax expenses: When it comes to life's major expenses, are you addressing these costs pretax or posttax? Paying for large expenses before paying income tax helps you avoid the tax altogether. The opposite scenario—paying taxes on the higher income figure and instead using what remains after taxation to cover these significant expenses—isn't nearly as wallet friendly. How do you score?

Create Future Tax Goals and Plans

The final foundational step for your pillars of tax planning is an actual plan. For this step, you must have a clear understanding of your future goals. Are you planning to sell your business in the next couple of years? Maybe you're considering purchasing a house or a second home, or your children will be heading off to college. Identifying these significant life events is the initial step so you can plan in broad strokes. Take the time to document these major milestones so that you can begin outlining rough plans.

Once you've outlined your future goals, anticipate potential obstacles. One common hurdle involves loans. If you're planning to purchase a house next year and intend to take out a loan, you may need to demonstrate higher income for a larger loan. This presents a dilemma, as it means paying more income tax when you need cash to buy the property. Obviously, that's not ideal.

It's only once you've identified your obstacles that you can start planning solutions. For example, when it comes to getting a loan and avoiding paying high income taxes, several fixes are available. The most common is to explore investments in other assets, such as a car or business equipment. If you finance an asset with minimal cash commitment compared to its value, you can then depreciate it entirely in the current year.

Let's say you're getting ready to buy a house, and you'll need a mortgage. The year before, you buy a business-dedicated vehicle or equipment for $50,000. You can deduct or depreciate $50,000 without immediately having to shell out that cash. This allows you to leverage the depreciation deduction to lower your taxable income—paying tax on only $150,000 if your income is $200,000. This lets you manage expenses and income to keep that cash for when you're making your down payment.

Once you have financial situational awareness, have projected your expected tax liability for the next year, and have outlined your overarching financial objectives, your proactive foundation is complete. At that point, you have your base built and ready. That's where the pillars of tax strategy come in.

The Pillars of Tax Strategy

The pillars of your tax strategy are built on four key components. Situational awareness forms the foundation; if you took the advice in the first heading of this chapter, you've probably already figured that out. In this section, I'll

Effective Tax Planning

Entity Structures

Deductions/Credits

Wealth Strategies

Situational Awareness

be introducing the other two pillars: (1) entity structures and (2) deductions and credits. Together, these pillars will collectively guide your approach to optimizing your financial situation, managing your taxes, and keeping more of your hard-earned money in your business or pocket.

Entity Structures

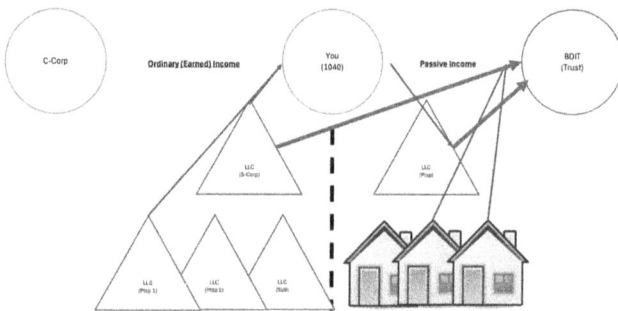

Entity structures refer to the legal structure of your business (S corp, limited liability company [LLC], C corp, and others). They can get quite complex, but many business owners opt for an LLC. The key concept here, whatever your entity structure, is to envision your income on two sides of the page. On one side, you've got ordinary and earned income; on the other, you've got passive income. I'll explain these in detail in this section.

Side 1: Ordinary and Earned Income—
Tax Considerations for LLCs versus S Corps
On the first side of the page, you'll account for anything categorized as ordinary or earned income—essentially where

your primary business income resides. This income is subject to self-employment tax unless you strategize carefully, and far too many entrepreneurs get hit with this nasty surprise. Self-employment taxes, sitting atop regular income tax, constitute 15.3 percent of any business income you generate. That can add up.

Let's say you've earned $50,000 in your first year of running your business. Before even thinking about income tax considerations, you're confronted with self-employment tax, which alone exceeds $7,500. This financial hit catches many entrepreneurs off guard. The solution to this bill lies in entity structures.

The LLC

For entrepreneurs engaged in more than just a temporary or seasonal business, especially when they have a continual and planned business strategy, establishing an LLC is crucial. An LLC provides flexibility and options for the future, and it's simple to set up. It's a typical starter entity structure for many reasons.

Without an entity structure, all kinds of issues can come up. Let's say you don't bother to create one. The next year at tax filing time, when you're looking for tax advantages and realizing you don't have an entity, you'll wish you had opted for one. Retroactively creating an entity and having it taxed advantageously for the past year isn't easy. The fundamental step is to open an LLC. If you haven't done that yet, consider it.

LLC, Then S Corp

One reason LLCs are so powerful is that they provide you with flexibility to switch entities, making it an excellent starter entity. Typically, entrepreneurs make the switch when their profits surpass a certain threshold, usually around $20,000 to $30,000. It becomes particularly important when your profit exceeds $30,000.

Suppose you're midway through the year—around June, July, or August—and you realize that your earnings are on track to warrant the benefits of an S corp. That existing LLC allows you to make a seamless transition; you can designate the existing entity as an S corp for the current year. That way, you get tax advantages without having to create a new entity mid-year.

Entity Structures for Multiple Businesses

If you're the sole owner of a single business, that's great—you only need one entity. If you own or want to start any additional businesses, they can be incorporated into that same LLC.

Entrepreneurs often find themselves involved in multiple businesses. You may very well be one of these people. At first, you might think, *An S corp worked well for the first one, so it should work for the second and third.* I suggest keeping it simple and limiting yourself to one LLC filing as an S corp. This is largely because of the burden of wages related to entity structures.

When operating under an LLC or an S corp, you're obligated to pay yourself a W-2 wage, subjecting you to self-employment taxes. If you have multiple S corps, each will require you to pay a wage. This not only results in more wages than desired but also introduces complexities because each S corp has its own unique rules and structures. By having your single S corp own all your other businesses, you can avoid this issue.

Entity Structures for Partnerships

Identifying the right approach to maximize your deductions, especially when dealing with partnerships, can be challenging. One partner is often inclined to enjoy luxury, such as driving a Ferrari, while the other partner might prefer the practical, like driving a Camry. Balancing both of these vehicles in the business and ensuring fairness between the two partners can get awfully uncomfortable.

Let's say you maintain a single LLC that files as an S corp. If any of your other businesses are structured as partnerships, your share in those businesses can be owned by your S corp rather than you as an individual. This way, everything funnels into your LLC. This approach simplifies your setup and enables you to manage your deductions more effectively within the single LLC, avoiding concerns about partnership dynamics or the need to ensure equity between you and a partner.

Side 2: Passive Income: A Second LLC

While there are various passive income sources, rental real estate stands out as a great example. We'll explore this further in a second, but first I want to impress on you that the key here is separation.

If you're a business owner, you would typically manage one LLC, usually an S corp, for your day-to-day affairs, like we discussed. Then you may have another LLC to hold your real estate ventures. Yes, I know I just said you only need one—passive income is the exception.

This second business entity is often a partnership, especially if you're married, although it may also be a wholly owned LLC. Either way, all income streams converge into a single LLC that you wholly own, preserving the control discussed in the previous section.

For this kind of arrangement, a series LLC—a parent or umbrella LLC with many branches—could be a good idea for enhanced asset protection. From a tax perspective, the objective is to allocate each property to its own LLC.

There are strategic reasons for maintaining a distinct LLC for passive income, especially if you plan to compensate your children for their contributions to the business. This strategy works well with a family partnership, but it faces hurdles in an S corp due to specific rules. Implementing this approach for the passive income side is a good workaround.

What Happens If You Have Income Levels above $350,000?

Once you start bringing home over $350,000 annually, the goal is to redirect that income away from your personal return to minimize your tax burden. The sheer tax rate becomes a concern at this point, reaching levels of forty to fifty cents on every dollar of income exceeding that threshold. To counter this, you need to shift some of that income off your personal return, and there are many ways to do that.

Passive losses: Explore ways to generate passive losses, especially if you have real estate assets. This may include accelerating depreciation on your real estate properties through a cost segregation study, like we discussed above.

Shift ordinary income to passive income: You can shift some of your ordinary income into the passive LLC to avoid income tax. You can do this in a few ways, including licensing intellectual property to yourself or renting a property you own to your business.

C corp: If you need to get more dramatic, you can create a C corp. This involves deferring some income from the LLC to a C corp, where it can be subject to a flat 21 percent tax rate. You can then do your investing within that C corp. You don't necessarily need to own every asset outright. Having control is enough. You own the C corp, and this C corp possesses various assets and investments that you control. Even if the money in the C corp exceeds what you would have had in your personal name or bank account, as long as you control it, you're good.

Trusts ($500,000 or more annually): Once you're making $500,000 annually, you can start looking at trusts. Trusts can be leveraged as a method to offset ordinary and passive income against each other. This comes into play when you reach the limit of what can be achieved by shifting income between different entities.

I've generalized these concepts, and I'd be happy to discuss them further with you if you think they would work for your business.

The Entity Structure Breakdown

Our approach to entity structures gets a little complicated at the end. But if you boil it down, you're left with two main points:

Establish an LLC for your ordinary operating business: Keep it streamlined by having one LLC for your primary business. You should wholly own this LLC. If you have other businesses, integrate them into this single LLC that you entirely own.

Segregate passive activity: Create a separate LLC for any passive activities, especially if you're dealing with rental real estate or other passive income streams.

This dual-LLC structure allows for clarity and effective management, separating your active business operations from passive income activities. This simplified approach provides a solid foundation for many entrepreneurs.

Deductions and Credits

Most people earn their income, then allocate a significant chunk (ranging from 20 to 50 percent) to taxes, leaving them with their after-tax income. From that, they cover their housing, transportation, groceries, travel, and more, and whatever remains is what they can put into savings and investments. This is exactly why we're typically looking at that thirty- to forty-year time horizon for retirement. The math gets downright scary, especially for those in their forties, fifties, or sixties, who may be thinking, *How can I pull this off when I don't have four decades ahead of me?*

But that doesn't have to be the timeline for us entrepreneurs. We have options and, frankly, some incentives that are built into the tax structure. We can move some of our normal expenditures into business or deductible expenses.

Most people ask, "Can I deduct this?" I want you to ask, "*How* can I deduct this?" Framing the question around eligibility is a mistake. The focus should be on strategizing how to make a deduction legally feasible. We can do that with proactive tax planning in a variety of areas.

Proactive versus Retroactive Tax Planning

For a deduction to be legal, it must be both ordinary and necessary. I had a client years ago who was a great example of proactive tax planning. This guy was a dentist, and he wanted to purchase a tractor for $60,000. A tractor is neither ordinary nor necessary for a dentist's office, but the dentist owned the building housing his practice and was paying a landscaper for maintenance.

To deduct the tractor, we created a workaround. The dentist established a family management company to oversee the building. He then acquired the tractor through this company. Finally, he and his family took charge of landscaping for the practice. This made the deduction legal and aligned with the ordinary and necessary criteria.

For the dentist, the tractor was more than a tax-saving scheme; it became a source of enjoyment and stress relief. It also facilitated his new property management business, where buying such equipment was essential for day-to-day operations.

On the flip side, we have Laura. Laura is, as much as I hate to say it, a typical example of an entrepreneur who's late to the tax-strategy table. Laura and her husband have a plumbing business, and while that business was growing, they were paying more and more tax every year. They thought their CPA was thinking about this stuff for them, but that wasn't happening.

When Laura came to us in 2023, she had all her income—$170,000—reported as self-employment income. As a result, she was looking at a federal tax bill of $40,000. She was in Texas, fortunately, so at least she had no state tax.

Our fix? We set up an S corp and changed Laura's LLC to an S corp. Because she already had that LLC in place, we could go back and retroactively make that change. Luckily, she had done that much. That immediately changed her $26,000 in self-employment tax to $5,300 in payroll tax. Having the right entity in place saved her almost $17,000 in taxes.

We also had to deal with Laura's new Dodge Durango. Laura's accountant said she wouldn't qualify for a deduction on the vehicle since Laura primarily worked from home. Her husband drove a van to take care of the plumbing work. Her vehicle didn't have sufficient business use to make it deductible.

To fix the issue, we had Laura sign up for a mailbox service. This service, strategically located on her daily route for dropping off kids and running errands, allowed her to accrue business miles every time she checked the mail. By setting up this routine, we turned what was previously considered personal travel into a business-related activity. Even though part of the trip involved dropping off her kids, the return leg became a business-related journey. This allowed her to categorize 90 percent of the trip as a business expense. That deductible business expense saved her about $8,700 in taxes for that year, but we couldn't retroactively credit it toward the previous year.

We implemented other deductions, like an accountable plan, and leveraged tools like the Augusta Rule (which allows you to rent your home for up to 14 days without needing to report the income on your taxes). In the end, we reduced Laura's tax bill from $39,000 to $12,000 and change.

Laura lowered her tax bill by over $27,000 in a given year. It's so painful when you talk with someone in the same situation and they already filed their taxes. What a waste. Think about what $27,000 could mean for a business or even just for doing something nice for yourself, like taking a vacation.

Although we were able to salvage Laura's situation, you can see the difference between those two trajectories. Getting proactive with a strategy can make a difference of tens of thousands of dollars. If the dentist had purchased the tractor and went ahead and incurred landscaping expenses throughout the year, then asked us for help deducting the tractor, it would have been practically impossible. Correctly configuring the circumstances from the get-go is the only way to establish legitimacy and legality. Then, filing the tax return involves accurately reflecting what genuinely occurred. Attempting to retroactively alter events after the fact can land you in trouble. That's why Laura's savings on her new vehicle had to wait a year.

Common Deductions and Credits

Remember, the question isn't whether you can deduct but how you can strategically deduct. Here are some key areas to look at:

Your house: Deduct as much of your house as possible. I recommend going beyond the home office and into the Augusta Rule, which lets you rent your house to your business.

General real estate: Invest in real estate, accelerate the depreciation on it, plan to avoid getting limited with your passive losses, and plan for shifting income around between ordinary and passive income, preventing any roadblocks due to passive losses. This approach enables you to claim deductions for your real estate investments.

Cars: Incorporate cars into your business.

Recreational vehicles: Find a way for recreational vehicles to be ordinary and necessary in your business, like the dentist with his tractor.

College: Pay your kids to work in your business and then have them put that money into their own college savings account. You can then take a deduction for whatever you paid them for their work, and they can put that into their after-state-tax college savings, resulting in a second benefit.

State taxes: Determine if your state features the pass-through entity tax—a way to bypass the $10,000 state tax deductions cap imposed by the Tax Cuts and Jobs Act—and route the tax payment through the company rather than paying it personally. Bypassing the $10,000 limit is great for business owners facing substantial tax liabilities.

How Much Do You Overpay?

Based on what you've read so far in this chapter, how much do you think you're overpaying? What does your tax bill look like, and where do you think you might have opportunities to lower your taxes? What would happen if you took that amount you saved and invested it back into your business? When you reinvest that money into your own business, the potential return on investment tends to be significantly higher than what you can expect from traditional mutual funds.

In our businesses, returns of 30, 40, or even 50 percent on money invested are attainable. That adds up to major money over a short time. This is how we create a flywheel and momentum of wealth generation, allowing us to shrink the timeline down from thirty to forty years to less than ten.

This all starts with finding a good CPA, but don't blindly rely on an accountant or CPA; instead, you should seek to comprehend the strategies and rationales behind each step of tax strategy. It can feel overwhelming when this knowledge comes at you all at once, so it's tempting to leave it to the CPA.

Luckily, you don't need to know everything.

In this chapter, we'll tackle a couple of things you need to understand, and if you can grasp those, then you'll know enough to take the next steps toward great tax strategy. You can add on different pieces as you go. For now, condense your focus into the major areas that you need to think about. Then, as you grow, we can add complexity down the road.

Your ideal CPA depends on your unique situation, so that's where we should begin the conversation. My firm offers various services, and if they align with your needs, I'd be more than happy to discuss them with you. If not, we have established relationships with several CPAs I've collaborated with for years, and I can confidently point you toward the right fit.

6

Help from Experts

To be an entrepreneur, you have to know how to sell. If you don't know how to sell, you're a contractor. You might have a couple of clients, but you have no ability to control how much money you bring in. So to graduate from being a contractor or an employee to someone who can have a business, you have to generate sales. You have to say "I want to hit this sales target and this growth target" and then be able to go out and do it.

But what about when you go from being a small-scale entrepreneur to something bigger? You now have to get to another level—you've hit a point where there isn't enough human brainpower to hold onto everything that needs to be done. That's when you need help. If you want to scale your business—especially to cross seven figures in annual sales—you need to build a team that can act and think independently of you, and you need to know how and when to delegate to that team.

This chapter is about getting help from experts. I'm not talking about building your own expertise through education here—I'm talking about building your dream team. By remembering your role in the business, you can make sure to delegate at the right times and in the right manner. Then all you need is the right team to get the job done.

Your Role in the Business

Sometimes I find myself assisting entrepreneurs who have either too many or too few employees. My client James was in a huge amount of debt and had shut down his marketing agency, absorbing the debt in the process. When he came to me, he was back to being a solo entrepreneur.

James was a good salesperson, but he didn't want to have a team, and that limited what he could do.

"My previous team didn't have clear roles," James said during our conversation. "I assigned tasks haphazardly when they needed to be done. No one knew who was responsible for what."

"What if something wasn't getting done?" I asked.

"I'd just hire another person for it." He shrugged. "I'll be honest—it was kind of a mess." Labor costs had soared, and eventually, he had hit a dip in sales. The situation quickly spiraled out of control, forcing James to shut everything down.

James's issue was that he didn't understand his role in his own business. I keep saying this, but I can't say it enough: Nobody cares about your business and your money as much as you do. That's why you've got to know what's going on with your business and your money. Your hired help will continue to draw from your resources, be it through wages or fees, while you're left to deal with the consequences. It's not because they're out to get you; it's that nobody is as financially or emotionally invested as you are.

Like James, I used to be hands-off too, but I've learned that when I'm too relaxed, the team tends to be too relaxed as well. They know I'm not going to scrutinize their work and come at them with a critical eye. As a result, when I didn't set my expectations and then follow up—asking for details and pointing out flaws—I'm the one who ended up frustrated and on the hook.

You have to take ownership, period. Accountability is the role of the business owner. Being the CEO means understanding enough about every aspect of the business so that you can delegate responsibilities, get people to commit, and hold them accountable. If you're not actively engaged in reviewing your taxes, asking questions to gain insights, and examining your finances to seek understanding, then your accountants and bookkeepers can get lazy. You have to take care of the results since you're the one who's stuck with them.

With that in mind, let's talk about what and how to delegate tasks to your team.

What to Delegate

The general principle guiding delegation is to determine tasks that fall into either of these categories:

1. Tasks that someone can do more effectively than you can.
2. Tasks that you don't enjoy.

If handling your own bookkeeping on a Friday night while watching a movie is relaxing for you, then it's perfectly fine to continue doing it. I have a client who manages his own books even though he has no financial necessity to do so. He could delegate this task and likely use his time more efficiently. But he enjoys it, and obviously he's also invested in the results, so I don't think that's wrong.

Most entrepreneurs don't enjoy these tasks, so delegating them is often the wise course of action. Just make sure that when you delegate, you're not transferring ownership or responsibility; you're assigning the execution of the task.

How to Delegate

A few years back, I had new floors installed in my house, and the flooring salesperson assured me that the installer was "one of the best." When the man arrived, I said, "Go ahead. Do your thing." Busy with other things, I didn't inspect the work before I signed off and he left. Afterward I noticed defects and issues that led to a series of inconveniences, including trips back to the store and additional expenses. It wasn't a great experience, but I learned from it.

What would have happened if I had been more interested in the installer's work? If I had set the expectation up front that I would thoroughly examine the work and not sign off on it until I was satisfied? The installer would have checked his work more carefully before presenting it to me for approval. I still wouldn't have needed to micromanage the process or create a detailed installation guide for him— he's the professional; he knows his job. He needed to be aware that I would hold him accountable. I delegated the task poorly and ended up with poor results.

We covered delegation in chapter 4, but this chapter will give you an actual process for effective delegation. Delegating boils down to three crucial steps. If you follow these, people will understand that you will hold them accountable. They'll be motivated to ensure the task's success, and if they need to prioritize something, they will prioritize your tasks.

1. Clear Communication of Expectations

Once you've decided to delegate a task, be clear about the desired outcome. You and your team need to be on the same page about what the output is supposed to look like. What does "good" look like? What does "bad" look like? You need to agree.

The desired outcome may require some additional knowledge on your part, and that's your responsibility. You have to understand enough to make it clear what outputs you want. If you have questions about the kind of outputs you want concerning finances or taxes, refer back to chapter 3 or chapter 5.

2. Support and Information

Allow individuals the opportunity to ask for clarification and obtain the information they need to effectively deliver the task. Be sure to respond to them promptly.

3. Follow-Up and Accountability

Follow up to ensure that the task is delivered as expected. When the work is delivered, review it to hold individuals accountable for their responsibilities.

Your Experts

Now that we've discussed the concept of delegation, let's talk about the folks you'll primarily be delegating to—your team. I'm not talking about your general employees here. I'm referring to the specialists, usually contracted out to start and then perhaps brought on full time, who bring you the expertise you need to make your business run smoothly.

Insurance and Legal Counsel

New entrepreneurs who are cautious about their expenses and reluctant to spend often fail to notice the many insurance and legal considerations involved in running a business. It's essential, however, that things are set up correctly and well protected.

Establish a long-term relationship with someone who can serve as a single point of contact for insurance and legal counsel. A trusted legal or insurance expert over the long term can guide you through all the fine print. Your insurance rep will safeguard your assets and limit your liabilities, while your lawyer will properly structure agreements and anticipate potential issues, such as legal disputes, payment collection challenges, or the threat of legal action. These are the intricate details that experts specialize in but are easy to overlook.

Developing a relationship with trusted experts in these areas can save you a significant amount of time and headaches over the years. Remember to maintain a good understanding of what's happening. Don't allow anyone to sell you on an insurance plan or product you don't fully comprehend.

If you're serious about your business, make an initial investment of a few thousand dollars to have a lawyer evaluate your business. Working with lawyers is advantageous since their services usually aren't an ongoing expense. That one-time payment can reveal critical issues, while also establishing a relationship where you can return for assistance as needed. Lawyers can serve as an annual physical checkup that identifies and addresses problems before they escalate.

Bookkeeper and CPA

Your bookkeeper and your CPA may share an office, but their jobs are quite different. They're often not the same person because the individual who excels at strategic thinking doesn't typically excel at bookkeeping.

Your bookkeeper's primary responsibility is to ensure the accuracy and timeliness of your financial records. Everything they oversee pertains to the past—your historical financial data. They don't analyze, and they don't strategize. But they do pride themselves on the details.

Your CPA's primary role is strategic in nature. Everything they oversee pertains to the future. They should be capable of analyzing, interpreting, and transforming your financials into actionable insights. They often have a team to ensure the accuracy of the financial data, but their core function is to look ahead, especially in terms of tax planning. They consider your wealth goals and the broader financial landscape, then provide guidance on tax strategies and future financial planning to avoid potential issues down the road.

Your CPA is important, but they shouldn't take the central coordinating role between other professionals, like lawyers, unless your CPA is also your CFO. In general, you are the CEO, and everyone should report to you. Maintaining a flat organizational structure in this regard often leads to more effective results.

Managing Your Team

Managing a team is a skill. For some entrepreneurs, that kind of leadership comes naturally, while for others, it does not. One resource that has been helpful as I built my team-leading skills is the book *Traction* by Gino Wickman,[6] recommended to me by my client Will, the marketing entrepreneur from chapter 4. If you're struggling with your leadership skills, I can't recommend this book enough.

Getting into the details of team management is outside the scope of this book, but I want to leave you with one more piece of advice. As you manage your team, everyone must be on the same page in terms of both macro and micro expectations. As we discussed in chapter 1, it's important to differentiate between micro (short-term, smaller) results and macro (long-term, ultimate goal) results.

Let's examine this in terms of your CPA. Yes, your CPA should have a clear understanding of what you expect from them on a monthly or annual basis, and you must have this discussion up front to align your expectations. But it's equally imperative that your CPA be aware of your long-term objectives for your business, as driven by your well-defined dream of success. This not only keeps you focused but also ensures that your CPA comprehends the broader, long-term goals. Long-term goals can, after all, influence short-term outcomes. So always ask your team to keep the big picture in mind when making smaller choices.

Help Them Help You

One of my clients once said to me, "Find a really good number two who can help implement all the ideas you have

---

6   Gino Wickman, *Traction: Get a Grip on Your Business*, United States: BenBella Books, 2012.

in your head." You may indeed need to bring on a CFO like this as you grow, but this concept also has a broader application. No entrepreneur started a business because they love to deal with money, legal red tape, or bookkeeping. But if you're passing these tasks along to hired help, you need to ask yourself some necessary questions. Will this team recognize that you genuinely care? Do they know you will scrutinize the tax return, ask questions about areas you don't understand, prod the reasons behind certain decisions, and show a sincere interest in their work?

Once your expert team perceives this commitment, their behavior toward you changes significantly, and you'll receive a higher level of professionalism. If you remember your role as the business leader and delegate the correct tasks in the correct way to the correct experts, you're setting yourself up to scale your business and hit that seven-figure mark.

7

You

I won't lie—this chapter gets a little philosophical, and it was fairly difficult to write.

My wife and I enjoy exploring the topic of personal growth, but we don't always align on which voices appeal to us. The ones I prefer to listen to sometimes don't do much for her. There's some crossover in that Venn diagram, but something that means a lot to me might fail to resonate with her.

So I encourage you to take this chapter with a grain of salt. You may need to pursue personal-growth content on your own, and you'll find the things that mean something to you. On the other hand, maybe you'll like some of my musings, in which case I'm glad to have shared them. With that in mind, this chapter is all about you—why you're here, both as a person and a business owner, and how you can keep growing and improving throughout your personal and professional life.

The Meaning of Life

This book is about entrepreneurship, but there aren't a lot of people who, on their deathbeds, would think, *That sale I got really mattered.* In some sense—not to be depressing—nothing we do here on Earth matters much. Everything we do as entrepreneurs will fade into obscurity, our businesses may fail, and any wealth we pass down to our children will likely be squandered—perhaps within just a few generations.

Entrepreneur and author Seth Godin spoke about this very topic, the seeming long-term futility of our professional toils, on his podcast, *Seth Godin's Startup School.* He asked, "Are we all rearranging deck chairs on the *Titanic*?" and explored the idea of whether we behave like hysterical passengers or like the small orchestra playing music as the ship sinks. Does it ultimately matter whether we give up and panic or choose to do something meaningful, even if we all eventually end up in the same place? According to Godin, the answer is "maybe."

I think the fact that we will all, someday, be forgotten shouldn't stop us from trying right now. The musicians who provided a sense of normalcy and peace amid the chaos of the sinking *Titanic* left a lasting impact. We remember their actions because they held meaning, even though they didn't

---

7 Seth Godin, host, "The Dip," *Seth Godin's Startup School* (podcast), December 17, 2012, accessed November 4, 2023, https://podcasts.apple.com/us/podcast/the-dip/id566985370 /.

prevent the tragedy. Those musicians chose to stay and do their best, and that choice carries significance. What we can draw from this is to strive to be the best we can be, regardless of the circumstances.

Here to Grow

Family, personal integrity, living a good life, being good to people—these are the things that matter in the world. I look at them from a religious point of view, but from a secular perspective, think of it as leaving the campsite cleaner than you found it. The way you use your time matters—you can waste it or give it everything you have, squeezing every drop out of it. But the ultimate reason for our existence is to develop, grow, and become better each day. And, interestingly enough, I believe entrepreneurship is one of the best ways for us to fulfill that meaning.

Yes, this does have a literal application in the form of business growth. As a business owner, you have to continue pushing the boundaries. That doesn't necessarily mean top-line growth, but you should always be trying to make your business better. The same thing goes for us as people.

I hit a point in my career in my early thirties where I was making a lot more money than I had ever expected. At that young age, I had reached the goal on how much money I wanted to make in my career per year. If you had asked me ten years earlier how much I was aiming for, I was there. But—surprise—I wasn't happy.

A lot of people go through that; it's kind of the classic midlife crisis. I asked myself, "Do I want to keep doing this for the next couple of decades?" And that sounded terrible to me—monotonous, boring, and meaningless.

What I eventually came to—the idea that gave me peace—is that it's not about the money. It's about growth. No amount of money can replace the pursuit of accomplishing something that's hard to accomplish. That's the thing that forces us to grow, and growth provides meaning, especially because it tends to improve our lives and the lives of those we touch.

Your Business's Impact

As business owners, we touch a lot of lives, and the aspiration of making a positive difference on others through my businesses has always been a driving force for me. The question is, Can you establish a business that not only benefits you but also becomes a net positive in the lives of your team members and customers? A place where people will be grateful to have crossed paths with you on their journey?

This doesn't have to be anything huge. Not everyone needs to aspire to make grand, globally scaled advancements. The simple and everyday activities we engage in, like running a marketing agency that helps other businesses increase sales, or owning a store that provides people with essentials, can make a difference.

There's also your team. By treating team members with respect and helping them grow to achieve their personal aspirations, we become a part of their journey and personal growth. Not every action needs to be extraordinary and headline-worthy. It's about excelling in the ordinary things and inspiring and leading others in a way that holds intrinsic meaning and value.

Growing as a Person and Entrepreneur

Becoming the best version of yourself is a complex journey unique to each of us. The first step isn't just about mastering the specific skill of delegating but acknowledging your shortcomings as an entrepreneur and taking responsibility for overcoming them. Once you know what you're missing, you can work to improve yourself while still appreciating what you have.

Recognizing Weaknesses

I'm not great at detailed work, especially reviewing tax returns. Initially, I tried to suck it up and do it myself. Then I attempted to delegate, but the results were mixed. The problem persisted until I realized that it wasn't merely a matter of delegation or doing it myself. The problem also wasn't with the person I delegated to. It was my delegation skills that needed improvement. I was the problem. As the owner and founder, I had to be a better leader, manager, and communicator. I had to acknowledge that the ultimate responsibility lies with me.

I'm definitely not alone in this regard. Your own capabilities often limit your business's growth, but this is the beautiful challenge of entrepreneurship because it compels you to keep growing.

Recognize that all businesses, no matter the size, have flaws. From small mom-and-pop shops to giant multinational corporations, no institution is perfect. This realization might be surprising, but it's true. People are flawed, so businesses are too.

Perfection isn't the goal.

The question is whether you accept this challenge, aiming to improve, or shy away from change, limiting both yourself and your business.

As small business owners, we often become bottlenecks, not only in workflow but also in terms of knowledge and leadership. Your inability to lead effectively may limit your business in various areas, like sales, hiring, communication, or financial control. For owner-founded businesses, particularly not venture capital startups, the onus is on you to overcome these challenges and address your bottlenecks.

You don't need to be perfect, because perfection is unattainable. Owning up to your flaws, however, and finding ways to improve are essential. In my case, the shift in perspective was empowering and challenging. It's easy to blame others, but taking responsibility and recognizing that I needed to address the problem—whether through better delegation, hiring, or leadership—made a significant difference in my business's growth.

Limitations Aren't Weaknesses

Sometimes the limiting factors in your life may not be weaknesses at all, and you don't need to apologize for them or change them.

I have four kids, and quality time with them and my wife is a top priority. I can't follow the advice of childless entrepreneurs who work incredibly long hours or wake up at four o'clock in the morning. I need to spend time with my family, so my daily routine has to adjust. I'm content with waking up at six o'clock instead of four o'clock.

I've learned not to take advice too literally, especially from those without kids. It's not that I disregard it entirely, but I've learned to adapt advice to my own circumstances. You'll need to do the same.

Improving Yourself: Lifelong Learning

Your current skill set has made you the bottleneck in your business; it's time to do something about it. A lot of people like to attend conventions or conferences, and you can certainly devote time to that. This section, though, will focus on one of my favorite ways of taking in new information: reading.

The Importance of Reading and Executing

Reading is absolutely important to me. Sure, there are those who refuse to read anything, especially self-improvement books, claiming, "Self-help books won't help me achieve anything." A kernel of truth exists in that perspective, I suppose, though the real truth is more nuanced. Reading is essential, but not to excess. Reading is the starting point that exposes us to new ideas. "Read too much, and it can become counter-productive—you feel like you're accomplishing something, but you're just treading water." You're stuck in a loop of ideas, and you have to push yourself to take action. Spending all your time reading to gain a solid theoretical approach won't get you anywhere.

Alex Hormozi emphasizes that it's better to read the same book five times and implement it than to read five mediocre books one time. You have to read, and then you have to take action before picking up the next book and forgetting what you read in the last one. The right balance involves both reading and implementation. You read to get new ideas, and then you have to do something.

Five Book Recommendations

I found the following five books to be particularly meaningful for my own personal growth and addressing my flaws.

Eat That Frog: 21 Great Ways to Stop Procrastinating and Get More Done in Less Time by Brian Tracy: I found this book helpful for addressing common struggles with time management. It can transform an entrepreneur's sense of overwhelm into a sense of purposeful action.

High Performance Habits: How Extraordinary People Become That Way by Brendon Burchard: Useful for knowing when to quit in your work.

The Dip: A Little Book That Teaches You When to Quit (and When to Stick) by Seth Godin: I found this book valuable for deciding whether to abandon a challenge or embrace it, helping you focus your energy where it matters most.

The One Thing: The Surprisingly Simple Truth behind Extraordinary Results by Gary Keller: Another helpful resource for general personal development.

The Dichotomy of Leadership by Jocko Willink and Leif Babin: This book emphasizes the need to be decisive while considering other options, especially in leadership. It's about finding the balance between strong leadership and listening to your team's opinions. In many situations, finding the right balance is essential. Conveying this balance doesn't always translate well in a book, but it was still worth the time.

Appreciating What You Have

I recently had a day at work where my computer wasn't cooperating, the internet wasn't connecting, and I was falling behind on important tasks. I left work, frustrated, already late for a family event, and found myself stuck behind a slow driver.

I'm so worked up, I thought. I decided to pause, reflect, and gain some perspective. I reminded myself of the blessings in my life: a thriving business, a comfortable car, a healthy family.

Gratitude. It's about recognizing the goodness in our lives and appreciating it, which helps us avoid dissatisfaction, anger, or frustration. Even if we have weaknesses to acknowledge and improvements to make, we can be grateful for where we are and how far we've come. Negative emotions are all too common, but life is far more enjoyable when we remember to be grateful.

The Business of Living

Entrepreneurship serves as a platform for lifelong learning and enables a more significant impact on others. And, when done effectively, entrepreneurship can lead to personal financial freedom. As an entrepreneur, you may already know this. If you're not experiencing these benefits from entrepreneurship, it might be time to reassess.

Business owners often find themselves caught up in a whirlwind of busyness, which can be overwhelming. This is where taking a step back becomes crucial. Remember that you're making a substantial difference in the lives of your clients, your employees, and your community. You have numerous opportunities for continual learning and self-improvement. Don't forget to savor the personal financial freedom that comes with it.

Viewed through the correct lens, our businesses and our satisfaction with life, in general, depend on our willingness to persevere and accept that we only succeed to the extent that we develop. We're only going to feel successful—not be successful objectively, but feel successful and feel like we're living productive lives—to the degree that we can look in the mirror, have honest conversations with ourselves, and recognize our weaknesses. If you can do that and commit to continuing to grow and develop, then you'll be able to overcome or open up the various bottlenecks through different stages in your business. If you remember what's important, you can find meaning and satisfaction in your life as an entrepreneur and as a human being.

Your Next Step toward Bottom-Line Profits

You're probably reading this book because you want to make some kind of improvement in the financial aspect of your business. I hope that you've found something that you can take and use to improve, and now that you've found it, take action. Like I said in chapter 7, if you read a book and make no changes, what's the point?

Feeling overwhelmed and don't know where to start? Pick one thing—the first thing, your worst pain point—and take action. If you can do that, if you can get one thing that you implement out of this book, then the time spent reading and learning will be worth it for you.

If you need help or would like to talk about if and how we can help you on the journey, you can schedule a free consultation. See my website at brianbbasinger.com for more information.

Bibliography

Hormozi, Alex. "Read 1 Good Book 5 Times." YouTube video, 0:24. June 25, 2023. https://www.youtube.com/watch?v=8J881zhJsp4.

Godin, Seth, host. "The Dip," *Seth Godin's Startup School* (podcast). December 17, 2012. Accessed November 1, 2023. https://www.globalplayer.com/podcasts/episodes/ZoghKA/.

"My Wife and My Mother-in-Law. They Are Both in This Picture - Find Them." n.d. https://www.loc.gov/pictures/item/2010652001/.

Brunson, Russell, host. "The Drifter vs. the Driven and Live Q&A with Russell." *The Marketing Secrets Show* (podcast). June 20, 2022. Accessed August 29, 2023. https://marketingsecrets.libsyn.com/the-drifter-vs-the-driven-and-live-qa-with-russell.

"Study Shows Small Companies May Have Overpaid Taxes."
n.d. https://www.govcon.com/doc/study-shows-small-companies-may-have-overpaid-0001.

Tracy, Brian. *The 100 Absolutely Unbreakable Laws of Business Success*. United States: Berrett-Koehler Publishers, 2002.

Wickman, Gino. *Traction: Get a Grip on Your Business*. United States: BenBella Books, 2012.

About the Author

For more than a decade, Brian Basinger has been helping his entrepreneur clients lower their taxes and achieve financial freedom and security without pinching pennies.

Early in his career, Brian recognized that large companies and top entrepreneurs are able to maximize their profits and minimize their taxes because they can hire experts who help them take advantage of every possible loophole.

Brian believes that new entrepreneurs and small business owners deserve that same kind of expertise. He has fallen in love with small business ownership during his own entrepreneurial journey and loves helping others succeed on their path to entrepreneurial success.

Brian lives in Utah with his wife, Pamela, their four kids, and three dogs.

www.ingramcontent.com/pod-product-compliance
Lightning Source LLC
Chambersburg PA
CBHW021458180326
41458CB00051B/6869/J